MIKE SMALLEY

The
YOUNG
EVANGELIST

Handbook

THE YOUNG EVANGELIST HANDBOOK

Copyright © 2002 by Mike Smalley

Unless otherwise indicated, all Scripture references are from the King James version of the Bible (KJV).

ISBN: 0-9712249-6-X

Cover Design: Joe Potter, Potter Design *www.joepotter.com*

Acknowledgments

---

*To Amber Summers, my personal assistant, for her
many hours of proofreading and typing the manuscript...*

*To Kristi Smalley, Jimmie Rouse, and Sue Mifflin for their help in
proofreading the book...*

*To Margaret Roark for excellent work in editing and formatting the
publication and making it ready for the printer...*

Honor Roll

---

*The following individuals and churches made
the printing of this book possible. I encourage all
who are benefited by this book to call their names in prayer.*

Jim and Donna Bruno

Pastors Rick and Rita DuBose

House of Grace Church-Ft. Worth, TX

Pastor and Mrs. Andy Jacobs

Anthony and Betty Lockaby

Metroplex Heating and Air Conditioning-Dallas, TX

New Horizons Fellowship-Rockwall, TX

Roy and Mary Norman

Rebecca Palumbo

Sachse Assembly of God Church-Sachse, TX

Dennis Schnell

Eric and Sheri Smalley

James and Toni Smalley

Pastors Garry and Barbara Smith

Table of Contents

Foreword

W e are living in days of extreme spiritual famine. The starving masses, all over the world, are crying out for fresh bread and fresh water. For those in ministry, these are the days of unprecedented opportunity. Christianity has what the world is crying out for, but there is a problem. There's too much to do, and not enough workers to do it. There are plenty manning the storehouse, but so few slinging the sickle. Everyone wants to enjoy the reward of the harvest, but not many are willing to bring it in.

My prayer is that God would quickly call and equip thousands of young men and women. We are in desparate need of Blood-washed, Holy Ghost-inspired, clean-living, on-fire, itinerant servants of the Lord. In short, we need evangelists, and we need them now. My friend, there is no time like the present. The fruit is ripe on the vine. We must bring in the harvest while it is day. If not, it will rot in the fields.

Mike Smalley has written a timely book for all those who sense the urgency of the hour. This is not an 'encyclopedia set' on how to be an evangelist, but rather a practical hands-on manual to help you navigate through the waters of early ministry. Having served in both roles, as pastor and evangelist, Mike has gleaned valuable experience, and can offer sound advice to those with a listening ear. Avail yourself to the well-learned lessons of someone who has walked this road.

Be assured, there are landmines in the road ahead. The enemy desires nothing more than to steal your joy, kill your enthusiasm and destroy your effectiveness. Regardless, the young evangelist must be willing to forge ahead with cautious determination. May this book serve as a compass as you embark upon the adventure of a lifetime.

Young evangelist, here is your handbook.

– Stephen L. Hill, Evangelist

Preface

I love preachers. I love evangelists.

One of the blessings of my life is encouraging the pastors for whom I preach.

One of my passions is to help mentor young people who feel called into the ministry. Being an evangelist, I am especially called and burdened to do what I can to equip and encourage young evangelists.

When I began as a full time evangelist, I found myself totally ignorant on how to begin and build an effective evangelistic ministry.

This frustration has been used by God to develop the book you are about to read. It does not contain everything you will ever need to know. However, it does contain enough information to help you begin and build a solid and powerful ministry as a young evangelist.

The office of the evangelist is needed now more than ever before. My prayer is that God will use this book to launch thousands like yourself into the harvest fields of the earth as an effective, anointed, and fruitful 21st century evangelist!

To all God's evangelists -
past, present, and future...

CHAPTER ONE

The Evangelist

God is radically in love with the human race.
God's dream is a world of people like Christ.
God accomplishes this by the new birth.
(see John 3:3; II Corinthians 5:7)

———

People who have experienced this new birth are discipled, loved, corrected, and trained in the local church.

"For God so loved the world that He gave His only begotten son..." (John 3:16) and God so loved His church that He *"gave some apostles, some prophets, some evangelists; and some pastors and teachers;"* (Ephesians 4:11)

The most visible of Jesus' gifts to His church is often the local pastor. Most individuals feel they have an accurate understanding of what a pastor is and does. Very little confusion exists on this issue.

But what is an evangelist? What does an evangelist do?

Many have asked such questions and I've heard several different responses. Thankfully, the Bible answers this question.

Before we give the definition of what an *evangelist* is, perhaps we should go over what an evangelist is not.

A New Testament evangelist:

- is not an entertainer
- is not a singer (though an evangelist may sing)
- is not simply a traveling speaker
- is not a second-class preacher
- is not merely a businessman
- is not a pastor who is between churches

The word *evangelist* is found in the scripture three times, and only in the New Testament.

"...and we entered into the house of Philip the evangelist..." (Acts 21: 8b).

"He gave some to be apostles, prophets, evangelists, pastors, teachers..." (Ephesians 4:11a)

"...do the work of an evangelist..." (II Timothy 4:5).

The Bible says the evangelist is to *"equip the saints, for the work of the ministry"* (Ephesians 4:12).

The Bible also shows us the role an evangelist plays in preaching to the lost (see Acts 8).

An evangelist's ministry is a perfect mirror of the Great Commission given in Mark 16:15, *"Go ye into all the world, and preach the gospel to every creature"* and Matthew 28:20, *"Teaching them to observe all things whatsoever I have commanded you..."*

The English word for evangelist comes from the Greek words *euangelizo, euangelion* and *euange-listes.*

Euaggelizo means to "announce good news, or glad tidings" (Strong's Concordance 2097). This speaks of what an evangelist does. Jesus is THE Great Evangelist. This word is used over 40 times in the New Testament. Jesus was a preacher of good tidings (see Matthew 11:5; Luke 8:1).

Euaggelion means "the gospel or good message" (Strong's Concordance p. 2098).

Euanggelistes means "a preacher or messenger of good news" (Strong's Concordance p. 2099).

Scripture clearly shows us that the evangelist is a gift from Jesus to the church and to the lost.

I believe the proper definition of an evangelist is:

> *He is a gift minister from Jesus to His church, who obeys the great commission by equipping the saints and enthusiastically delivering the King's message of salvation and deliverance with such anointing and authority that his message demands attention, reaction and response.*

The History of Evangelists

The history of evangelists is a priceless heritage. Think for a moment of the impact this gift of Jesus has made on this and past generations.

First of all, Jesus functioned in the role of the evangelist, as did John the Baptist. Mark was called an evangelist by historians and the twelve disciples functioned as evangelists.

Down through church history, many men (and women) have made powerful impacts on their generation.

St. John Chrysostom preached during the Middle Ages, yet his preaching is discussed to this day.

In the 18th century, John Wesley shook England and gave us the Methodist church. George Whitfield was a powerful evangelist who helped bring about America's first Great Awakening.

In the 1800's, men such as Charles Finney, D.L. Moody, and A.B. Earle were used by the Holy Spirit to usher millions into the

Kingdom of God.

During the 20th century, William Booth birthed the Salvation Army, and individuals like Billy Sunday, Smith Wigglesworth, and Maria Woodworth-Etter made a lasting mark.

The evangelists of the 1950s, such as T. L. Osborn, Oral Roberts, A. A. Allen and Jack Coe, brought a wave of healing to the United States and the world.

And, of course, only eternity will fully reveal the fruit of modern-day evangelists such as Billy Graham, Steve Hill, Ray Comfort, Reinhard Bonnke, and others of our generation.

Yes, Jesus gave a powerful gift to the world and His church when He gave us evangelists.

It is impossible to have a proper and healthy New Testament church without the impartation, influence, and contribution of evangelists.

Can you imagine Jesus walking toward you with a beautifully wrapped gift? As He brought it forward, you could not help but see the love in His eyes and the holes in His hands and feet.

Imagine now you're leaning forward and slapping His gift of love to the floor and angrily stomping on it while shaking your finger in His face and screaming, "I don't *want* your gift, I don't *need* your gift!"

I do not know of a single Christian who would consciously do such a thing. But isn't that what the church world does when we ignore what the Spirit is saying through this gift called the evangelist?

One of the reasons that many congregations have turned inward and shifted their focus off the Great Commission is the growing number of churches which neglect to allow an evangelist into their pulpits.

Yes, the evangelist is a great and needed gift. To be called to be an evangelist is one of the greatest honors a Christian can receive.

Does your heart burn for lost souls? Do you get angry that the church is not better equipped to make the Great Commission the great completion? Allow the Holy Spirit to speak to your heart. Perhaps you, too, have this call on your life to follow in the footsteps of Jesus, John Wesley, and Billy Graham.

Maybe you were set apart in your mother's womb for such a time as this. Maybe you are called to be *A New Testament Evangelist!*

CHAPTER TWO

The Call of an Evangelist

The Holy Spirit is actively at work today calling individuals into full-time ministry. God is actively raising up evangelists all across the world.

God called me into the ministry when I was fourteen.

I was recently ministering in the West African nation of Ghana. I had just finished preaching and had come off the platform when I was approached by an enthusiastic, happy young man. He introduced himself as someone who felt God might be calling him to be an evangelist. His fire and zeal were very real.

This young man is a reminder to the body of Christ that the Holy Spirit is raising up a generation of preachers to help bring in the harvest. You are no doubt reading this now because you know or suspect that this call is on your life.

Many young people have questions about how they can know the will of God. How do you know what God wants you to do with your life? Asking the Holy Spirit to reveal His will for your life is one of the most valuable and necessary prayers a Christian can pray. God will answer.

Seven Questions to Ask Yourself Concerning the Call of God Into Full Time Ministry.

1. Has God spoken to you about full-time ministry?

"My sheep hear my voice and I know them and they follow me" (John 10: 27)

2. Has God "made you to know"?

Many ministers (including this evangelist) would be unable to explain how they knew they were called to preach. Many have used the phrase, "God has made me to know." If you know in your "knower," as one preacher has said, then you know that you're called to preach. I knew so deeply that I was called to preach that there was not an individual alive who could convince me otherwise. God simply "made me to know." I have that same conviction to this day.

3. Do you know in your heart that you would never be happy doing anything else?

If you can be happy and content in another occupation, that is a clue that you are not called into the ministry.

4. Do others close to you confirm or sense that you may be called to preach?

I do not believe that God calls people into the ministry through personal prophecy. The Bible says that God's sheep hear *His* voice. When God calls an individual into the five-fold ministry as listed in Ephesians 4:11, He speaks to that person *directly*. I believe God will use other believers to confirm the call that He has *already* given. Never allow an individual to "prophesy" you into the ministry when you have no heart for it or direct word from God yourself.

5. Do you have an interest in reading books on the ministry and sitting at the feet of those in ministry?

If a person tells me he is called to preach, and yet he never goes to a seminar, he never seeks opportunities to sit at the feet of ministers, and he has no interest in reading or learning about the ministry, then I do not think that person is called to the ministry.

6. What angers you? Anger is a clue to your calling.

Do you have a passion for the lost? Do the consequences of sin, both in society and in people, anger you? Do you have an inner compulsion to address it? Do you feel anger rise up within you when you see the divorce rate rise, murders increase, etc.

7. If you feel that you are called, have you been to see your pastor?

Make an appointment with your pastor and share your heart with him. Get his advice; obtain his counsel. Share in detail what you feel God has been saying to you and where He may be leading you. Get his feedback. Based on your age, ask him what he recommends you do next. You will not be wasting his time. Approach your pastor with confidence.

These questions, answered honestly, will help you to prayerfully establish whether you are called to preach or not. Having been in full-time ministry for many years, I can say that there is no greater honor or privilege than to preach the Gospel. I am asking God to give me a long life, and I intend to use that life for the glory of God.

While the ministry is both rewarding and fulfilling, it is also lonely, difficult, and painful at times. Anyone genuinely called into the ministry would be a fool to reject that call. On the contrary, to enter the ministry when you are not called is equally foolish.

It is important to remember that God seldom, if ever, reveals all of His plan for our lives at one time. God's will is revealed to us in stages, based on our obedience and faithfulness in our present circumstance.

When God called me to preach at the age of fourteen, I knew without a doubt that I was to spend the rest of my life in full-time preaching ministry. It would be several years before I knew that I was an evangelist.

Eight Important Actions For Every Person Called Into The Ministry.

1. Make an appointment with your pastor.

Ask your pastor to recommend some evangelists whom you might interview concerning the beginning of your ministry. Share with him your willingness to serve in any area of the church. Let him know that you want to begin your ministry *now*, by serving under his leadership. Ministry always starts now, not later.

Many young people make the mistake of "waiting until they're ready" to begin a ministry in their local church. There is no such place in life. How could any of us ever be totally qualified and prepared to be a representative and ambassador for the King of kings and the Lord of lords? Who could truly ever be prepared for that? Remember that God uses us to minister even during our times of preparation.

I remember as a young man having an incredible yearning to preach, but very few pastors knew me. I was asked to preach only once or twice a year. However, I constantly read and stayed active in my local church. I was working *toward* the ministry I now have, but

I was just as much in the will of God during my preparation as I am now in fulfilling my assignment.

An important part of being a church evangelist is the ability to bless, encourage, and serve a pastor. Some pastors see evangelists as takers and not givers. Cultivate the habit of serving, loving, and supporting your pastor and the pastors for whom you preach. Begin now with your home pastor.

2. Go where pastors are.
Ask your pastor to keep you informed regarding local meetings where pastors gather, such as pastoral lunches, ministers' meetings, and prayer breakfasts.

Visit different denominations in your city when they have their state meetings. Get to know as many pastors as you can. Introduce yourself as a person who feels called to be an evangelist. Relationships are the key to unlocking the doors of future opportunity. God will reward your efforts. Never be pushy, but never be intimidated or shy about pursuing the call of God on your life. If you don't share your heart and make pastors aware that you are available, how will they know?

3. Attend every church service you can.
Attend your church faithfully – every time the doors are open. Stay informed through your local newspaper of various guest speakers that other churches are bringing in, whenever your church is not meeting. Attend all the revivals, conferences, and seminars that you can. *Invest in your own future.*

4. Establish a daily prayer and Bible reading schedule.
Leonard Ravenhill said, "No man is greater than his prayer life." Begin now to develop your prayer life.

You should begin every day in prayer with God. The secret of praying is praying in secret. As you mature, and your ministry grows, you will find it easier and more necessary to spend extended amounts of time in prayer.

You may find spending extended periods of time in prayer right now to be very difficult. Don't let the enemy put a guilt trip on you. Set a certain time every morning to get up and a certain time every night to go to bed (this is important). Dedicate at least fifteen minutes *alone* with God every morning, and then allow the Holy Spirit to extend that time.

Many believers have been discouraged from a fruitful and productive prayer life because they feel that if they don't spend hours a day in prayer, there is no point in pursuing the Lord. God does understand and allows us to begin small and to grow. Remember, it is hypocritical to preach prayer to others when you have no prayer life of your own.

5. Observe and document the practices of successful evangelists.

Have a filing system where you can file your notes and easily retrieve them later for further study and growth. Remember – information that is not retrievable is not useable.

Watch evangelists on television. Learn from them. How do they promote their ministry? How do they make an altar call? How do they communicate what they are doing? How do they share their vision? How do they receive an offering?

Become a student of evangelists. Become a student of great men of God. When you attend a church service, take notes on how the evangelist runs his ministry table in the hallway. How does he set it up? What pictures does he have on it? What books does he have? Does he have a tablecloth? How does he conduct himself from the pulpit? How does he mention his ministry table? How does he preach? *Take notes meticulously on everything.*

6. Interview as many evangelists as possible.

Call evangelists and arrange phone appointments with them. Meet in person with those who are willing to meet with you. Have a list of questions *before* you call. Carry a cassette recorder to record their answers (with their permission, of course). Ask their advice on how to get started. Make your questions specific on a wide variety of topics.

Never assume that an evangelist will not make time for you. While you will not succeed in getting appointments with everyone you contact, always make the attempt. I've been turned down by many men of God in the past, but have found *most* more than willing to give me time. What would I have missed if I had assumed they were not available?

7. Obtain formal training.

Do everything possible to attend a Bible School. Until you are able to do this, take advantage of the many correspondence programs through the internet or postal service. One way or the other, allow those who have gone before you to impact your life. Jesus prepared thirty years for a three-year ministry. We prepare three years for a thirty year ministry. There is no way to estimate the value of sitting under the ministry of men and women of God in a Bible school setting. The relationships that you will build there will bless you for a lifetime.

Remember, success in the ministry is always based on relationships. Get to know as many people as you can, and allow as many people as you can to know you.

8. Read, Read, and Read some more!!!

Reading is *crucial* for growth in the ministry. Reading is *vital* to your development.

One noted minister said many years ago "If you're not going to read, get out of the ministry."

Charles Spurgeon said "If you will not make use of the brains of other men, it proves you have no brain of your own."

Begin now to establish a healthy library of books. Read biographies of successful men of God, evangelists, and pastors. Read books written by the Puritans. Read books on finances. Read books on leadership. Read books on family relationships. Read books on time management. Read books that deal with your particular area of calling and interest.

You are responsible for educating yourself in the areas in which you are ignorant. Make it a goal to read at least two books a month. Begin now.

I will forever be thankful to God for allowing the blessing of soul-changing books to come into my life.

For a list of "must read" mentorship books for the next twelve months, please contact our office.

CHAPTER THREE

The Evangelist and His Mentor

Every person God calls needs mentors.
A mentor is any person from whom you learn.

You will have mentors you've never met. By listening to cassette tapes, reading articles and books of that particular person, they will mentor your life and thus your ministry. There is no substitute, however, for an individual who knows you. I put this type of individual above an unknown mentor. I call this individual a spiritual father. Every preacher needs a spiritual father – someone who knows your strengths, understands your weaknesses, acknowledges yours fears, and believes in your vision.

A spiritual father is someone who will have a great influence on your life and will love you *where you are, but not as you are.* A spiritual father could never leave you like he found you. A spiritual father will not be afraid to rebuke you when you need it and praise you when you deserve it. A spiritual father's heart is to always leave you better than he found you.

Five Things to Look for in a Spiritual Father

1. Has God joined you to that person?

Special relationships like a spiritual father can't be forced. You can make yourself available to people, but you can't demand that they feel a certain way about you. When God places a spiritual father in your path, that person will have a sense and a drawing toward you, and you toward him. Again, it is important to note that a spiritual father is *not a peer*. A spiritual father is a *father*. He is a father in the spirit in the same way he would be old enough to be your father in the natural.

2. Is he a preacher?

If you're going to be an evangelist, you don't want a spiritual father who is a banker. Remember, you can be discipled as a Christian and mentored by people in various occupations. You can learn from Christian businessmen and others not in full-time ministry. However, you need a *spiritual father* who is in and understands the ministry. Ask God for a spiritual father who understands *your type* of ministry.

I consider the need for spiritual fathers to be the most critical need in the church today for young preachers. Paul told Titus, *"Let the older women teach the younger women"* (Titus 2:4). Paul was giving a principle here that applies to both men and women. The older are to teach the younger.

Remember Solomon's son, Rehoboam, who had the kingdom torn from him because of a decision that he made to listen to his peers rather than heed the counsel of those who were older (see 1 Kings 12).

Proverbs 27:10a says, *"Thine own friend, and thy father's friend, forsake not..."* This tells us that we should respect the wisdom of older generations. *Remember time and experience has not made you equal.* Never allow yourself to be deceived into thinking that church life has changed so much in the past twenty-five to thirty years that men of that generation have nothing to speak into your life.

You will ignore the former generation at your peril.

3. Is he willing to spend quality time with you?

To be a spiritual father is to give a great investment in time. A man who wants to meet with young preachers only once a year is not a spiritual father to anybody.

4. Is this person trustworthy?

Can you trust him with your life, your ministry, and confidential matters? Does he have a reputation of being able to keep matters confidential, or is he known as a gossiping preacher? If he is critical of other ministers or of highly visible ministries, that may be a negative clue.

5. Does he have your best interest at heart?

Many years ago, I came home for Christmas from Bible school. My father shared with me that a retired pastor had recently conducted a revival meeting at my home church and that, by coincidence, the man lived some ten miles from my home. I had never heard of this man although he had lived this close to me for ten years!

My father suggested that I make an appointment with him while I was home on Christmas break. My father had discerned the wisdom of God in this man and recognized that I needed such a man in my life. I was reluctant to contact this man of God since we had never met, but I will always be thankful to God that I listened to my father's counsel.

I obtained the man's telephone number and called him. I introduced myself as a Bible College student temporarily home for Christmas. I asked him if while I was home, I could buy him breakfast or lunch and ask him questions about the ministry and the things of God. He replied that he would be glad to do that, but unfortunately was leaving the next morning to attend a "Prayer and Bible" conference in another state. I thanked him for being willing anyway and we hung up.

Ten minutes later my phone rang. It was the man of God calling me back. He said, "I don't know why I didn't think about this a moment ago, but I'm actually going to this conference alone. If you would like to ride along, I would be glad for you to go with me." That was the weekend that I met my spiritual father. This man had my best interest at heart. That weekend changed my life. I will never forget the ride in the car to Oklahoma. I had never heard such truths, such wisdom. I had never heard such meat for my soul as this man poured into me, a young man whom he had never met.

That was over ten years ago and to this day, my spiritual father, James Morris, is a vital part of my life and ministry. I never do anything on a major basis without discussing it with him, and I never go more than a few days without contacting him by telephone or arranging to meet him for a meal.

I give God all of the glory for what He has allowed me to do with my life, and I know without a shadow of a doubt that my ministry could have been shipwrecked many times in the past had it not been for the guiding counsel of a spiritual father.

If you feel there is one chance in a million that you are called into the ministry, stop right now and ask the Holy Spirit to join you to a spiritual father. Pray this prayer:

"Heavenly Father, I thank you that you speak to your servants. I thank you for the call of God on my life. I acknowledge my need for a spiritual father. I believe that you have called me and are preparing me for ministry now. I believe that you have called and put into place a spiritual father for my life. I ask you to begin the process of revealing this person to me now. Reveal me to him and join us together for your glory and for your kingdom. In Jesus' name- Amen."

CHAPTER FOUR

The Function of the Evangelist

Considering Philip

To better understand the function of an evangelist in the New Testament, we must look at the life of Philip. He was called an evangelist in Acts 21:8.

Philip started his ministry as a deacon at the church in Jerusalem. He met the requirements of a deacon outlined in Acts 6 and was full of the Holy Spirit and wisdom.

Paul said in 1 Timothy 3:13 that those who use the office of a deacon well, *"purchase to themselves a good degree, and great boldness in the faith which is in Christ Jesus."*

God saw Philip's faithfulness as a deacon and called him to be an evangelist. You can be sure Philip's life involved hard work and travel. This, however, did not keep him from being the priest of his home. Philip understood the foolishness of trying to reach other people's children for Christ while neglecting your own.

Philip's four daughters were not only Christians, but they

prophesied (see Acts 21:9).

I believe that Philip's life and preaching were intentionally included in the pages of Holy Scripture for guidance to those who would follow in the office of evangelist.

Acts chapter 8 describes for us the role of the evangelist.

I believe an evangelist should be like the man Leonard Ravenhill describes in his book *Why Revival Tarries* as a man who, "will tell the devil no, who will storm the devil's stronghold, who will deny himself good food or good company or good rest, that hell may gaze upon him, wrestling, embarrassing demons, liberating captives, depopulating hell, and leaving in answer to his travail a stream of bloodwashed souls."

20 Scriptural Observations Concerning the Life of an Evangelist

1. The ministry of the evangelist is often a traveling, international ministry (Acts 8:5). *"And Philip went down to the city of Samaria (Acts 8:26-27).* God often joins people from different nations to the evangelist.

2. An evangelist is to preach Christ. *"Philip went down to Samaria and preached Christ"* (Acts 8:5). An evangelist is not to preach strictly about Christ, he is to *"preach Christ."* An evangelist does not come to simply speak *about* God. An evangelist speaks *for* God.

3. The evangelist's preaching is accompanied by such anointing and authority that people's attention is obtained and held. *"And the people in one accord gave heed unto those things which Philip spoke"* (Acts 8:6). Charles Spurgeon said, "You and I must continue to drive at men's hearts until they are broken. Then we must keep preaching

Christ crucified until their hearts are bound up."

4. The ministry of the evangelist is often accompanied by miracles. *"And the people with one accord gave heed unto those things which Philip spoke, hearing and seeing the miracles which he did"* (Acts 8: 6).

5. The ministry of the evangelist stirs up demons. *"For unclean spirits crying with a loud voice, coming out of many who were possessed with them"* (Acts 8:7).

6. The ministry of the evangelist is often accompanied by the gift of healing. *"And many taken with palsies and that were lame were healed"* (Acts 8:7).

7. The ministry of the evangelist produces great excitement and joy. *"And there was great joy in that city"* (Acts 8:8).

8. An evangelist's ministry will attract a variety of sinners involved in major strongholds. *"But there was a certain man, called Simon, which before time in the same city used sorcery, and bewitched the people of Samaria, giving out that himself was some great one"* (Acts 8: 9).

9. The evangelist makes his preaching believable. *"But when they believed, Philip preaching..."* (Acts 8:12). Charles Spurgeon said, "Believe what you do believe, or else you will never convince anyone else to believe it."

10. The evangelist preaches the whole counsel of the word of God. *"Philip preaching the things concerning the kingdom of God and the* name of Jesus Christ..." (Acts 8:12a).

11. The evangelist's ministry calls attention to water baptism.
"...they were baptized, both men and women" (Acts 8:12b).

12. The evangelist's ministry may change locations quickly.
"And the angel of the Lord spake unto Philip, saying, 'Arise...'" (Acts 8:26a).

13. The evangelist obeys now and asks questions later. "And he arose and went..." (Acts 8:27a).

14. The evangelist's ministry may expose him to those in great authority. "And behold, a man of Ethiopia, an Eunuch of great authority under Candace, Queen of the Ethiopians, who had the charge of all her treasure" (Acts 8:27b).

15. The evangelist has a constant listening ear to the voice of the Holy Spirit for new instructions. "Then the Spirit said unto Philip, Go near, and join thyself to this chariot" (Acts 8:29). I remember on one occasion when I was buying fuel for my car and I had already paid and gotten back into the car when I felt the Holy Spirit speaking to me to go back in and give a gospel tract to the man at the counter. I was in a hurry, I was busy, and I began to drive away. I had driven a short distance down the road and the inner compulsion to go back was not leaving. So I turned the car around and went back. I told the man I was a Christian and a customer and, though I had just left (as he well knew), I felt the Lord direct me back into the store to give him a tract. I have no idea what happened from there. I just know I went to bed that night knowing that I had done the will of God.

16. The evangelist has studied to show himself approved and thus can fulfill the scripture's commands, *"...be ready always to give an answer to every man that asketh you a reason of the hope that is in you with meekness and fear"* (1 Peter 3:15b).

17. The evangelist not only preaches to crowds, but he is also an expert at one-on-one evangelism. *"...and heard him read the prophet Esaias, and said, Understandest thou what thou readest?"* (Acts 8:30b).

18. The evangelist pursues the loner. *"And Philip ran thither to him..."* (Acts 8:30a).

19. An evangelist knows how to lead someone to Christ on a one-on-one basis. *"And Philip said, 'If thou believest with all thine heart, thou mayest.' And he answered and said, 'I believe that Jesus Christ is the son of God'"* (Acts 8:37).

20. The evangelist takes advantage of every opportunity given to him. *"But Philip was found at Azotus and passing through he preached in all the cities, till he came to Caesarea"* (Acts 8:40). An evangelist preaches Christ everywhere he goes, no matter how long he's there, and believes God for favor, fruit, and families.

Philip is an example of what a New Testament evangelist *should* expect in his ministry.

CHAPTER FIVE

The Launching of an Evangelist

Every evangelist should function out of a local church.

When you believe that you are ready to launch your ministry as an evangelist, consult with the spiritual authorities in your life. Do your pastor, your circle of mentors, your spiritual father (assuming he is not your pastor) feel that you are ready?

Ask your pastor to have an anointing and commissioning service, where he and the elders of your church anoint you with oil, lay hands on you, and send you forth.

Eight Vital Steps To Help Launch Your Ministry

1. Develop a quality brochure that describes you and your ministry.
This is one of the most important tools for an evangelist. A graphic artist should be hired to design this for you unless you are gifted in

this area. You shouldn't be afraid to spend money on a brochure. This should be done with the highest excellence possible. Your brochure should be in color, contain your picture, the ways that a pastor could reach you (your address, web-site, phone and fax numbers), a description of your ministry, and a list of ministry references (the more well-known the better) who would recommend you as an evangelist.

Your brochure should answer the following questions:

(a) What makes your ministry unique and different from that of another evangelist? and

(b) What would you hope to accomplish if you came to their church?

If your ministry is to preach revivals or to teach on soul-winning or encourage people toward missions, then your brochure should state that. There should also be a section in the brochure that deals with finances, accommodations, and travel arrangements.

If you would like a sample of our brochure or if you would like a list of Christian graphic artists and printers in the United States who could help you design and print a brochure at a reasonable price, contact the *Worldreach Ministries* office.

I recommend that you print a minimum of 500 brochures on your first printing. One of the dangers of printing too many brochures at one time is personal circumstances and information can quickly change. By printing in modest quantities such as 500, you eliminate the problem of having too many brochures so that if there needs to be a change or improvement made, you can do so within a reasonable time frame. There is nothing more frustrating than to print 5,000 of anything only to have it sitting in a box for three years until you can "get rid of it."

2. Get business cards printed, containing relevant information.

It is a good idea to have your picture put on the business card. People will remember your face when they have forgotten your name. However, if that is not possible, a quality business card with no photo is better than no business card at all.

Remember that information that is not retrievable is not usable. So always have something on your person that a pastor can access later. Never go anywhere without your business cards and brochures. Put some in your automobile. Put some in your briefcase. Put some in your jacket pocket. You never know who you are going to meet.

3. Once you print your brochures and business cards, they must be distributed.

They could be mailed out or handed out in person. A young evangelist should never be too proud or intimidated to approach a pastor with confidence and dignity, present material about his ministry and offer his service to a local congregation.

E-mail is also a good way to promote and keep in touch with pastors regarding your ministry. I recommend that you mail a letter of introduction and a brochure to a pastor after you do the following:

• Learn the pastor's first and last name and how to spell it correctly.

• Confirm that you have the correct mailing address for the church.

- Use a stamp – don't use a postage meter.

- Hand-write on the envelope in blue ink.

Your handwriting should be as professional as possible. I recommend putting your *address only* at the top left-hand corner and not your name. Remember – at this point, most pastors will not know who you are. Pastors receive numerous letters weekly. Create curiosity with your letter by not identifying yourself on the envelope. The letter must then be opened and your brochure and letter will take over from there.

4. Get a letter of recommendation.

Ask your pastor to write a letter of recommendation on your behalf and to provide you with a list of pastor friends to whom you could mail your promotional material. Your letter should be followed by a phone call after the pastor has had sufficient time to respond to your letter. Seven days is a good waiting period.

5. Call churches.

This is the most humbling way to secure a meeting. Be prepared to be turned down by many pastors until they get to know you. Be ready to be told by many church secretaries that you cannot speak to the senior pastor. Don't be discouraged! This is part of sowing the seeds of your name, with the expectation that your harvest will come. *"A man's gift maketh room for him, and bringeth him before great men"* (Proverbs 18:16).

Remember that a pastoral contact typically takes 6-12 months to materialize. The best day to reach a pastor is Wednesday. Mondays and Fridays are the worst.

An even better approach than calling is to have a letter with the pastor's name on it, along with your brochure. Go to the church and introduce yourself. Present your letter and brochure, and *leave* quickly. You may stay longer if the pastor invites you to do so.

6. Introductions to pastors.
Ask your pastor to introduce you in person to as many of his minister friends as he is able.

7. Preaching opportunities.
Preach wherever God opens the door for you. In the beginning of your ministry, you may be invited to speak in places such as Christian school chapels, youth group services, and nursing homes. It may be some time before the Lord gives you access to adult congregations, but learn to celebrate every invitation that you receive.

Remember what you are thankful to God for is what He brings more of to you. What you respect is what you will attract. If you are thankful to God verbally for invitations, then you will begin to receive invitations.

8. Help new evangelists get services.
Remember the principle of Ephesians 6:8. *"Knowing that whatsoever good thing any man doeth, the same he shall receive of the Lord whether he is bond or free."*

Mike Murdock says, "What you make happen for others, God will make happen for you." The scripture is clear that we reap what we sow. If you will help others to receive invitations and access to pastors, God will make the same thing happen for you.

Important things to Remember:

- Expect *some* (not all) pastors to seem disinterested in your ministry. Remember, you are not called to everybody.

• Ask pastors for whom you preach to call three of their pastor friends and recommend you. Then contact those pastors a week after that pastor has made the initial contact.

• Be anointed! By living holy, by being prayed up, and by preaching the Word, you allow the Spirit to move mightily in your services. Pastors talk. Nothing will promote you like a move of God in your services.

• Expect open doors. Remember, *"A man's gift makes room for him and brings him before great men"* (Proverbs 18:16).

CHAPTER SIX

Tools of the Trade

*Every evangelist needs "tools" that will allow him to
equip the saints and reach the lost.*

I recommend that as the evangelist is financially able, the following equipment be purchased:

1. A micro-cassette recorder.

Every evangelist needs to carry with him a micro-cassette recorder and keep it with him constantly. When God gives him sermons, ideas, etc., he will be able to record it immediately, so that he can use his mind and spirit for creativity and not for memory and storage. Successful people put into use their God-given ideas. What is not recorded or written is usually forgotten. Demonstrate to God your gratefulness for the ideas and visions that He gives you by being willing to document them immediately. We are stewards of the ideas that God gives to us. Document them. Have a system to revisit them. Have a plan to act on them.

2. A quality tape duplicator.

This needs to be one of the earliest pieces of equipment you purchase. It should duplicate a minimum of three tapes at a time and come in a portable case, making it easy for travel on airplanes and in automobiles. A tape duplicator will enable an evangelist to multiply his ministry to others by making cassette tapes available. In addition to the blessing this machine will be to those that you minister to, it will create needed revenue for your ministry over the years.

3. A PC or laptop computer.

You will need the ability to store financial records such as offerings and donations given to you by individuals. A computer with the appropriate software is an excellent way of maintaining your financial records. Don't skimp on record keeping. You will regret it if you do. You will also need a means of maintaining your growing mailing list.

4. A quality printer.

This will be an invaluable investment which can be used for newsletters and correspondence. It should be of a size that is easily transportable so that you can always take it with you.

5. A portable cassette tape or CD player.

It is so important to keep the atmosphere of the Word of God, the Bible on tape or Christian music continually going in your motel room when you're on the road. To do this, you will need a small portable cassette recorder. Keep the TV off! Motel rooms are depressing and abound with temptation. I recommend you spend as little time as possible in your room. I find working out of the local library preferable to spending time in a motel room.

6. A photocopier and a fax machine.

A photocopier will be needed for your office records, photocopying checks, and other ministry related items. Next, a fax machine, which will enable you to communicate quickly with those your ministry is in contact with. I suggest buying a combination copier/fax/printer which will be cheaper than buying three separate units.

Until your ministry is financially able to purchase these items without a burden, take advantage of office supply stores and develop a paper system for your mailing list and record keeping.

CHAPTER SEVEN

Financing the Evangelist's Ministry

Every evangelist needs money.
Every dream requires money to fulfill.
Every goal requires money to be reached.

———

Money opens doors that God intends for you to walk through. Lack of money will slam the doors of ministry opportunity in your face.

The speed by which the Great Commission is fulfilled, I believe, is determined more by finances than by the number of workers willing to go.

Every pastor needs money to grow his church. Every missionary needs money to reach his nation. Every evangelist needs money to fulfill the call of God on his life and to complete his assignment.

Money is not in Heaven. Money is only on the *earth*.

Thirty-eight of Jesus' parables are recorded in the scripture. Sixteen of them either dealt with or involved money.

F. Nolan Ball, in his book *God's Plan for Financing the Ministry*, writes, "If we understand that the bottom line determining success or failure in almost every project we undertake is, 'Can we come up with the money to adequately finance it?' then we will understand the extreme importance of financing the ministry."

5 Power Keys Every Evangelist Must Know About Money.

1. Money is the vehicle God uses to advance the Gospel to the nations. Always has been, always will be.
No matter how much time an evangelist spends in prayer on a day-to-day basis, no matter how much time an evangelist spends in the Word of God, the airlines are not going to give him free tickets to preach the gospel worldwide. Motel chains are not going to let him stay free of charge because he "loves Jesus." Publishers and printers aren't going to do his books free simply because he loves God.

Money is God's means of exchange in this world, and the gospel's availability or lack of it is directly related to the amount of money that flows into and out of the hands of God's people.

An evangelist should never apologize or be embarrassed, ashamed or awkward about requesting and receiving funds to finance his ministry. If you can't believe in your ministry, then why should anybody else support it? If you've been called by God, you have a divine right to receive the support of God's people.

An important point to remember is:

"NO ONE OWES ME ANYTHING!!"

Missionary Jack Harris taught me this principle several years ago when I began my ministry as a missionary-evangelist. Memorize this and say it to yourself on a regular basis, and remember it for the rest of your ministry.

Any ministry that is sustained by the seed offerings of God's people has discovered that the very people they thought would support them do not, and the very people they never expected to support them do.

By understanding and establishing early in your ministry that no one owes you anything, it will be impossible for you to be offended when those you love do not support you.

Paul said in Philippians 4:15, *"Now you Philippians know also, that at the beginning of the Gospel, when I departed from Macedonia, no church communicated to me as to giving and receiving, but you only."*

This is amazing when you read in Acts 15, that Paul was sent out by the church at Antioch on his second missionary journey, and they *did not* support him financially. Only the church at Philippi did (Phil 4:15).

This means your sending church does *not* have to be your supporting church.

Syvelle Phillips, founder of Evangel Bible Translators, once told me, "God calls some people to be your friends, and some people to be your partners, and friends don't have to be your partners, and your partners don't have to be your friends."

An evangelist should never be lazy. He should always work hard. He should welcome and make opportunity for those who believe in his ministry to support it, while remembering: NO ONE OWES ME ANYTHING.

2. Money is not evil. It's the love of money that is the root of all evil (see 1 Timothy 6:10).

Someone said, "Money won't buy you happiness, but poverty won't buy you happiness either." Neither will it open doors for you to reach the nations for Christ.

3. Jesus needed money for His ministry.

Jesus needed money to support the twelve disciples. He called them away from their secular occupations and invited them to be "fishers of men." Can you imagine the expense of thirteen men traveling full time on the road? What about their lodging, food and clothing? We know that at least one of the twelve was married because the Bible mentions that Peter had a mother-in-law. This means that Jesus needed to generate enough funds to take care of not only the disciples, but also the needs of their families while they were on the road.

How was Jesus' ministry supported? *"And it came to pass afterward that he went throughout every city and village, preaching and showing the good tidings of the kingdom of God: and the twelve were with Him, and certain women which had been healed of evil spirits and infirmities, Mary called Magdelene, out of whom went seven devils, and Joanna, the wife of Chuza, Herod's steward, and Susanna, and many others, which ministered unto him of their substance"* (Luke 8:1-3).

The Greatest Evangelist understood the value of regular support. If you fulfill the will of God for your life, you will do no less. I am very aware that two are better than one, and a three-fold cord is not easily broken (see Ecclesiastes 4:12). My partners mean everything to me, and yours should to you as well.

4. You must be a giver to qualify to receive.

Every evangelist should be a tither. Every evangelist should bring 10% of his gross income into his home church. Certain denominations request that ministers credentialed with their fellowship pay a certain amount of their tithe to the headquarters office. I believe this is in keeping with scripture that the tithe is to be given to the ministry (see Numbers 18) and that it fulfills the scriptural practice of giving the tithe "away from one's self."

If you are not currently tithing, there is a curse on your finances (see Malachi 3:8,9,10). You will never have a successful ministry unless you tithe. God will not anoint a ministry that is stealing from Him.

Every time I bring my tithe back to God, I lay hands on it and thank God for what it represents. Then I claim the promise of Malachi 3:8-11, and ask God to make it a blessing to those who are receiving it, and I release them from the responsibility to report back to me on what they do with it. God will hold them accountable for how they spend it, and He will hold me accountable for bringing it.

Every evangelist should sow seed offerings on a constant basis to various ministries, including his home church.

One of the greatest discoveries I ever made in my life was understanding the principle of the seed. Genesis 8:22 says, *"While the earth remaineth, seed time and harvest, in cold and heat, in summer and winter, and day and night shall not cease."* 2 Corinithians 9:6 says, *"He which soweth sparingly shall reap also sparingly; and he which soweth bountifully shall reap also bountifully."*

Every moment of your life you are sowing a seed or reaping a harvest.

There are different kinds of seeds.

There are different kinds of harvests.

Clearly one of those is money. Since every evangelist needs money, every evangelist must sow money. You do not qualify to receive unless you give.

"Give, and it shall be given unto you; good measure, pressed down, and shaken together, and running over, shall men give into your bosom. For with the same measure that you meet withal, it shall be measured to you again" (Luke 6:38).

I recommend that every young evangelist sow seeds

into other ministries every month. The amount of the seed will be different as you're able and as the Lord leads. Remember 2 Corinithians 9:10 says, "He gives seed to the sower."

Never wait for a better financial day to start giving.

The Bible says God gives seed to the sower, not those waiting for better economic times. Start where you are. Start with what you have. The harvest that you need is created by the seeds you have now.

> *It is wrong for an evangelist to ask God for finances and to raise up partners to sow into his ministry, and not sow into the ministry of others.*

Galations 6:7 teaches us *"we reap what we sow."* By helping others achieve their financial goals, God will allow the same to happen to you. There are ministries that I believe in that I support because I know what I make happen for others, God will make happen for me. If you are seeking monthly partners, find someone else who needs monthly partners. If you're trying to build a church overseas, support someone else who is building a church overseas. If you're trying to write a book, help someone else who is writing a book.

Recognize that the Bible teaches that those who preach the Gospel should be supported by those who have already believed the Gospel.

Galations 6:6 says, *"Let him that is taught in the word communicate unto him that teaches all good things."* In other words, those who are learning should respond financially to those who are teaching.

I Corinthians 9:14 says, *"Even so hath the Lord ordained that they which preach the Gospel should live of the Gospel."*

In other words, people who have forsaken secular occupations to give their full time to the preaching of the Gospel have the right given to them by God to support their families and ministries through funds generated by the Gospel.

Numbers 18 teaches that God made a covenant with the tribe of Levi that would be an everlasting covenant. While the tribe of Levi and the other eleven tribes of Israel are not the authority of a local church today, it is the opinion of many, including this author, that those of the five-fold ministry mentioned in Epesians 4:11 are the New Testament version of the tribe of Levi in the Old Testament.

Jesus said, *"Ask and you shall receive. Seek and you shall find. Knock and the door will be opened to you."* We're waiting for people to be "led of the Lord" to give to us, and Jesus said, "Ask." It is scriptural to ask for help, support and partnership, and an evangelist should not be ashamed to do what is scriptural.

The Bible does not say, "Ask not, and it will be given to you. Seek not and you shall find. Don't knock and the door will just open for you." It says, *"Ask, seek, and knock."*

Every Christian is required to obey the Great Commission by participating in both going and sending others. God will take you places most cannot go, so you are providing an opportunity for people to sow seed into areas of the world that they could never reach and influence if not for ministries like you. People want to be a part of something bigger than they are.

I constantly communicate to my partners that whatever I do for God, they are right beside me in the mind of God. They are part of my family.

Recently, one of our monthly partners wrote me, sharing how excited she was to be a part of what our ministry was doing for God. She feels a part of our ministry family because I have regularly communicated that she is a part of it.

5. Understand that people are more willing to give than you are to ask.
Always remember this. Never make people's decisions for them.

Never assume who will support you and who won't, and never negotiate with a giver.

Your Three Main Sources of Income

There are several avenues of income on which an evangelist should focus.

1. Honorariums and offerings received from preaching.

2. Income generated from a ministry table at speaking venues, such as books, sermon tapes, videos, CDs, tracts, etc.

3. Money given by God's people in person and through the mail.

One area in which beginning evangelists normally have difficulty is discussion of the offering when they speak at a church. A standard policy for evangelists should be to request the senior pastor or host of the meeting to receive an offering for their ministry in every service in which they minister, including Sunday mornings. A church having two Sunday morning services would receive an offering in each morning service.

Many times a senior pastor, when approaching an evangelist, asks, "What are your financial arrangements with churches?"

I believe a God-honoring answer is, "Thank you for your interest in our ministry, Pastor. We do not charge or have a set fee for our services. We simply appreciate all our expenses being covered and an offering (never use the term "love offering") being received for our ministry in every service in which we minister."

Why is it important to request a Sunday morning offering?

• *Luke 10:7 says, "The laborer is worthy of his hire."*

No man would have a plumber work on Monday and Tuesday, and pay him only for the Tuesday labor. When an evangelist preaches on Sunday morning, that audience should have the privilege of responding in an offering as the Holy Spirit leads them.

• *The Sunday morning audience will be the largest audience both for the day and the week.*

I've preached in almost every major denomination in the world and have learned one thing about all of them: Sunday morning is still the most-attended service. To allow the largest crowd of the day to walk out without an opportunity to respond to the one whom God has used to bring His message is not right.

In the United States in the early part of the 1900s, when churches across America had far fewer financial resources then they do today, many times the offerings taken on Sunday morning went 100% to the pastor, and the offerings that were taken on Sunday night were used for other church-related expenses. This has translated down through the years into a mentality that the offering on Sunday morning is "for the church" and other offerings should be received on Sunday evening. *This is not scriptural nor practical.*

Having pastored for six years before I was a full-time evangelist, I can assure any pastor that a good offering for his own church can be received before the evangelist speaks. After the evangelist has preached, or after the altar call has been given, it is then appropriate to ask the audience to be reseated and to respond in an offering for the evangelist. Asking ushers to stand at the back door after a service rarely generates a financial blessing for the evangelist. Respectfully request that a normal offering be received.

Expecting the Monday night or Tuesday night crowd at a revival to "make up" in an offering amount for what the Pastor didn't give the Sunday morning crowd a chance to do is not fair to the people or the evangelist.

When an evangelist is ministering to a congregation for the first time, it is advisable to have the offering received after he preaches. God's people always respond best in their giving after they have heard a message.

What do you do if a pastor refuses to receive an offering for you on Sunday morning? In your early days, my advice would be to gracefully say, "Thank you for considering it anyway," and go ahead and preach. As your ministry develops and there are more requests for your ministry, you can be more selective as to who you go to and under what conditions you accept an invitation. Always remember, no matter what your decision, a Christ-like attitude is the *only attitude* that God can honor and bless. Every evangelist should remind himself that the senior pastor is not his source – only God is his source.

It is customary for the evangelist to turn the service back over to the pastor for the offering to be received at the end of a service. Certain churches may not be comfortable receiving an offering after an evangelist has preached, and in such cases, will want to receive the offering before the evangelist ministers.

When you find yourself in such a church, ask the senior pastor if he would allow you the opportunity to share with the congregation your vision and your ministry for a few moments *before* he comes to take the offering. Tell him that you would like to share with the people what their offering is going to help you do for the cause of Christ. Remind the pastor in love that no one can share another man's vision quite like that man himself.

There will be times when the senior pastor requests the evangelist to receive his own offerings. *This trust must never be abused!*

When a man of God turns his pulpit over to you, he is entrusting you with the highest honor he could give you. *Never* abuse that. Remember, your door into the congregation was through that pastor.

Never be afraid to confidently convey to a senior pastor your financial arrangements. You are a man of God. Your dignity matters.

Always do your best to have an understanding of the financial arrangements *before* you arrive at a church on Sunday morning. I recommend doing this in a letter. If you haven't settled the financial arrangement of a meeting before you arrive, it will almost always work against you.

Pastors hate surprises. So do evangelists. An informed pastor with integrity and a heart to serve an evangelist will not hesitate to discuss finances with you. Any pastor who tells you, "Oh, don't worry about the finances. We'll take good care of you," and refuses to discuss money with you in detail is very likely to be a pastor who will take advantage of you financially.

Proceed in speaking and working with such a pastor at your own leading. No senior pastor would ever be satisfied to meet with a deacon board before they hired him, and have that board refuse to answer his questions about finances. If the deacon board said, "Oh, brother, don't worry about finances. Just move your whole family here, and we'll worry about that when you arrive," no pastor in his right mind would do that.

No missionary would move overseas and not have any idea of how much support he could count on from his friends and partners at home. So an evangelist has a right to understand what the financial arrangements will be with the host pastor before he agrees to come.

The vast majority of senior pastors will do everything within their power to bless their guest evangelists. Take note of these pastors and publicly brag on them from the pulpit and privately express your gratitude.

> **Important Key:** *No New Testament pastor would be satisfied if the only funds he raised in his church were enough to cover his own salary. Why? He wants to build a ministry. He's not just there for income. The same is true for an evangelist. The offerings an evangelist receives are not for him, but for his ministry. A true evangelist will never be satisfied with merely enough money for his salary.*

Always remember that most senior pastors have never been evangelists. Most senior pastors have to be educated in love on what it is like to be an evangelist and to build an evangelistic ministry. You will hear such phrases in your ministry as, "Well, this check is more than I make in a week. It ought to be enough for you." You'll also hear things like, "Well, I wish it could be more." All of these will be frustrating words to an evangelist.

As the Lord allows you the opportunity, it is appropriate to share with pastors your ministry expenses, and *goals.* The average senior pastor typically thinks that the check he gives an evangelist is for one day or just a Sunday, but he doesn't understand that it's not a check for a day, it's a check for an entire week. What an evangelist receives on Sunday will be his preaching income for that week.

Another area in which most pastors are ignorant is they assume that the offering check they give an evangelist is for his salary. Many pastors don't consider that the check they give an evangelist is never for his salary. The check is for his ministry. Out of that check, he has to pay his staff, buy postage and supplies, keep a car in good running order, and maintain his office. Every typical expense a pastor has for his church office an evangelist has for his and more.

I have never met a pastor who had to consistantly pay the mortgage of his church out of his own salary, but every evangelist who maintains a public office must do that.

My experience is that most pastors are wonderful, Godly men whose hearts are to serve the kingdom of God and the evangelist. They will go out of their way to meet every need that you have, but along the way, there will be those who hurt you out of ignorance and yes, a few who may just rip you off.

Always remember that it is God who lifts up and prospers and God who tears down. Keep a Christ-like attitude. Never rebuke an older minister for what he has paid you or not paid you. You may succeed in getting a bigger check for the moment, but the devastation to your reputation as an evangelist can hurt you for years to come.

Remember, pastors, like evangelists, do talk. If a pastor hears that a friend had you for a meeting, he will ask that pastor how the meeting went. The recommendation that pastor gives, not his people, will often determine whether or not you receive an invitation to preach for his friend.

Ask the Holy Spirit to continually give you the wisdom to walk the fine balancing line of presenting your needs and allowing the Holy Spirit to bring the finances to you through the people that He wants, and not becoming a preacher who has developed a bad, non-cooperative reputation.

In instances where an offering may not be appropriate, such as a seminar or banquets, simply reach an agreement with your host on a satisfactory honorarium.

Other Financial Matters

Airfare Reimbursement

It is a common practice in the United States for the pastor who invites the evangelist to cover the expenses of the evangelist to get to his church and to his next destination. It is my recommendation that when you fly, ask permission of the church to book your own ticket, and then have the church reimburse you. This will put you in control of how many layovers you have, what time your flight leaves, etc.

Many a sincere but inexperienced church secretary has booked horrible flight itineraries for evangelists, causing many delays and wasted hours at airports.

When the above arrangement is made, always request that the church reimburse you for the airline ticket either by making the check out to your name or to the credit card on which you placed the plane ticket. Request two checks, one for your offering made out to your ministry, and the other for airfare reimbursement, made out to you. Every evangelist should seek to incorporate his ministry within his state and country. Among other benefits, this will allow you to give tax-deductible receipts to donors.

Fuel and Expenses

Many evangelists are hesitant to ask pastors to reimburse them for gasoline expenses. As a young starting evangelist, I would allow the Lord to lead you in this regard. There is nothing wrong with requesting that a pastor who invites you pay for your fuel and road expenses. However, keep in mind that every church should be considered differently.

Requesting a pastor of a church of 2,000 to pay your gasoline for a two-hour drive is foolish. However, if you drive eight hours to preach for the same pastor, that is a different matter. Always strike a balance between being a good steward of your time and your ministry resources and not looking cheap. When a pastor gives an evangelist a $2,000 offering, asking him to reimburse thirty dollars for gasoline is cheap. That's an open door never to be invited back. Receipts should always be presented whenever a request for fuel reimbursement is made.

Motels

I don't know of any circumstance in which an invited evangelist would be expected to pay for his own food or lodging while with a pastor. The expenses that an evangelist would incur while in a motel would be paying for his own faxes or long-distance phone calls. A church should *never* be expected to pay for such personal expenses. Always communicate in writing to the church before you arrive how your ministry check is to be made out and request that it be given to you immediately following your last scheduled service with the church. In the event that a church does not do this, for convenience sake, provide them with a pre-addressed, stamped envelope and request that they mail it to you the next business day.

Ministry Table

Every evangelist should believe enough in his ministry to carry his ministry products with him.

My golden rule for my ministry table is to never allow anything on it that I honestly do not believe will change someone's life.

I believe that my tapes, my books, and my tracts, when given to an individual and applied, will literally change his life and affect where he will spend eternity. You should feel the same about your material. Make available your sermon tapes, books or tracts, articles that you have written, CDs or music tapes that you have recorded or published, as well as sermon series.

The developing of these materials takes time and income; however, don't be afraid to get started. Some young evangelists are afraid to have a ministry table because they're embarrassed that there are only a few items on the table. Remember to start where you are and celebrate the small victories. If you only have one sermon series, take it to every church in which you preach. When you have two, take them with you. Put something out there for God to bless.

Never be afraid to let people purchase your materials. There will be times when the Holy Spirit leads you to sow your material free into the lives of the people, but always remember that it took time and money for you to write, produce, and market your products. There's nothing wrong with asking others to sow back into your ministry for your material, when it's going to be such a blessing to them.

There are people who will buy a car for fifteen thousand dollars, and yet the car never told them it loved them, and it never changed their life, never helped raise their kids, never saved a loved one's soul from hell. Yet these same people will complain to a man of God over the price of a ten dollar tape set that has the potential to change his world! So never be pressured into apologizing for making life-changing material available to the body of Christ.

Some ministries sell Christian T-shirts as a means of raising their finances. I do not believe this practice is wrong, and without a doubt, there is good revenue to be made from selling Christian T-shirts. I simply believe that as your ministry grows and matures, you must concentrate your focus on developing things centered around the word of God such as sermon tapes, teaching series, books, tracts, etc.

It is a good idea to include in your promotional packet a list of the items that will be on your ministry table, with instructions on how to contact you if there are any questions.

The Following Will Help You in Building a Quality Ministry Table.

1. Have every sermon taped.

There will be instances where this will be out of your control. Some churches' equipment will be broken or they will have no taping equipment at all. This is often the case in evangelistic crusades in rural outdoor areas. However, the vast majority of the places where you preach will have the means available to tape the services. Request that every sermon you preach be taped even if it is not the pastor's custom to tape his own services regularly. Provide the church sound man with a blank tape for each service, and instruct him when to start and stop recording.

2. On weekends when you are not invited to preach anywhere, devote your time to product development.

Spend a portion of your free weekends writing a book or gospel tract, preparing a cover for a cassette teaching album, or writing a sermon. By redeeming the time on these off weekends, you will quickly develop a book table that is a blessing both to you and to those who purchase your material.

I have a file in my office called "ideas" and another file called "book title ideas." When I have an idea for a future project or a future message, I jot it down or speak it into my micro-cassette player, and file it for later. It's amazing how in only a short period of time, you can come up with a large list of messages and articles to make available to others who are interested in your ministry.

Always remember there's no such thing as the perfect message. One of my regrets is that I did not develop my tapes earlier in my ministry. I was always waiting for the "perfect sermon" with the perfect delivery, and you and I both know that will never happen.

Develop something now.

Make it a goal to finish your first book within six months.

If you do not have a place to preach in the immediate future, develop a sermon by preaching into a tape recorder and make the message available.

Do your best when you preach and then sow it into the public arena and let God bless it. Make it available to people.

I recommend also that you give something away from your ministry table in every service you speak. Try to make it a different item every time if possible. When you are describing your material from the pulpit, always hold up a copy of each item so that the people can see it, then leave your ministry items on the pulpit until after the pastor has dismissed the service.

Your ministry item products are your presence somewhere else.

Your books and tapes will go where you can't go. They'll stay longer than you can stay. They'll talk to thousands on your behalf.

In the early days of your ministry, you'll find that the proceeds from your ministry table will make a difference in a week when you have nowhere to preach. It will make the difference in covering expenses you may have when you're on the road traveling to a church. All the items on your ministry table should be done with the best possible quality that you can afford. Quality tape labels, quality cassette album covers, quality tracts, quality books; all of these items should eventually be on your table.

Photographs of past ministry victories are also a blessing for people to see on your ministry table. Never underestimate the power of a picture.

3. Always ask a church to provide a table for you in advance of your arrival.

Let the church know the specific size that you need. Request that it be placed in a prominent and visible location such as the lobby of the church. I recommend having a trusted lady in the church to oversee the table for you, so you can give your time to praying with people at the altar.

Always bring a small amount of cash to make change, and have your ministry items and their prices listed so those looking and helping you will have the information they need. I do not recommend allowing people to take items off the table and mail the money to you later. Because you are a traveling ministry, it is too difficult to keep up with.

I recommend that as soon as possible, your ministry be set up to accept credit cards. You should display a small sign on your ministry table showing the credit cards you accept. You should also mention it from the pulpit. Also inform those working on your table in advance how individuals should make their checks out and make sure they understand how to handle the credit card charges. You should always sow something back into the lives of those who helped you work the table, such as a free tape. You may also consider making free copies of your live services available to those who work in the nursery or children's church.

4. Put your live messages on your ministry table.

One of the fastest ways to bless your ministry is to tape and make available your live messages.

When you arrive at a church, you will have brought your tape duplicator and several blank cassette tapes along with equal numbers of labels. The number of tapes and labels that you bring will be determined by the size of the congregation in which you preach. A good rule is to plan on 10-15% of the adult audience to purchase your tapes. When you arrive, present a blank master tape labeled with the date to the sound man.

Announce to the church that one of the ways in which they can be an additional blessing to your ministry is by purchasing your preaching tapes. Explain that the normal custom for your meetings is having all of the live services you preach taped and ordered from you at your table. They will pay in advance and there will be a sign-up sheet at the table so you will know who has placed orders. Before your last service, you will duplicate all the tapes that have been ordered. Place them on your ministry table to be picked up by those who ordered them. This is a fantastic way to bless your ministry and bless the people. I have never preached for a pastor who was offended by this practice. After all, they are your messages and your sermons and there's nothing wrong with you receiving the blessing from them as well.

As your ministry develops and takes you to even larger churches, time and protocol will probably not allow you to keep up with this practice. However, until such time, making live services available will be a tremendous asset to your ministry.

Finances Received Through the Mail

The most important avenue of income for the evangelist will come from his monthly partners. *Every evangelist needs monthly partners.*

Monthly partners are individuals who give to your ministry on a monthly basis. They will enable you to reach goals you could not reach without them. They will enable you to minister in other nations where you may not receive offerings large enough to support your budget.

They will sustain you during weeks when you are not asked to preach. They will allow your ministry to function with a budget of reliable income.

In short, they will partner with you to enable you to reach your dreams for God.

Always value a partner. *Always.*

7 Ways To Develop Ministry Partners

1. Make a list of every person to whom you would feel comfortable sending a Christmas greeting card.

This list should include friends, family, schoolmates, co-workers, and friends from churches you have attended. If you are married, organize a list from the people your spouse knows. Two hundred names should be a minimum starting place.

2. Obtain each person's current mailing address and phone number.

3. Write an introductory letter.

This letter should include their name and begin with some personal reference to your friendship. Briefly explain what you believe God has called you to do, and describe what your goals are and what your vision is. Make it *brief.*

Conclude the letter by sharing your need for partners. You are looking for partners who believe in the call of God on your life, who believe in the message that God has given you, and who have a heart to see the Great Commission fulfilled in our generation. Share in the letter what they can expect if they become a partner with you. Tell them what you intend to do for them. Examples of what this may include could be regularly praying for their prayer requests, sending free tapes of your messages, making your books and tracts available to them, etc.

Remind them that they can expect at least three harvests when they support your ministry. Those harvests would be "divine ability" (Deuteronomy 8:18), "divine favor" (Luke 6:38), and "divine provision for every need" (Philippians 4:15-19).

The letter should also include how they are to communicate back with you. It should include your name, address, telephone number, and an envelope for them to mail back the seeds that they want to sow into your ministry. It's also a good idea to put a return slip in it. Samples of these can be obtained by contacting our office.

Never ask for a "one-time gift." There is no such thing as an evangelist operating in the will of God who has a "one-time need." Ask people who do not wish to be your partner if they would sow a "special seed" into your ministry. Asking individuals to give a "one-time gift" puts you in an awkward position. If they give to you once, then ethically you cannot ask them to give again because you told them it would be "one time."

4. The most effective way to recruit monthly partners is a face-to-face visit.

There is no substitute for asking someone out to dinner, or to your house so that you can explain your vision. It is ethical to tell people up front what the purpose of your visit is. Briefly explain on the phone that you're looking for friends who believe in finishing the Great Commission, and who believe in you, to partner with a new ministry that God is calling you to.

If they tell you at this time that they are not financially able to support you, then tell them that you need to practice communicating and sharing your vision and would they allow you to come over anyway and hear what God has called you to do. You will find that many people will say yes and after hearing your heart in person, will decide to become your partners

Remember again the Golden Rule of ministry: No one owes you anything. So don't be discouraged if those you believed would support you don't.

Allow God to speak to whom He wants, but remember that God rewards our efforts. Sitting back and "waiting" for God to speak to people to support your ministry will most likely ensure that your ministry doesn't get off the ground. Remember, God is willing to speak to lots of people, but most people aren't still enough to listen.

5. Communicate with your partners monthly.

This is important. Don't feel pressured to exaggerate your ministry. Clearly, your friends and family understand that your ministry is just getting started. They don't expect you to preach to fifty thousand people every week, but they do expect you to be obedient to the call of God on your life. So simply share what God has allowed, burdened, and opened the door for you to do. Then share with them your candid progress on the matter. Always provide a self-addressed envelope for their convenience in returning an offering to you.

6. No thank, no bank.

I have tried to always abide by this simple but effective motto. It is both rude and inconsiderate to receive someone's financial seed into your ministry and not immediately thank them for it. If someone cares enough about the lost and believes enough in my ministry to send me something that represents their life, I as an evangelist should respond with a timely "thank you" and receipt. If your ministry is going to be based in the United States, I recommend you apply to become a 501(c)(3) non-profit organization as soon as possible. This will provide credibility to your ministry and allow donors to have a tax deduction for their gift.

7. Remember that you are in a covenant relationship with your partners.

Though it is geographically and physically impossible to speak personally with all of my partners on a regular basis, I communicate with them every month through our newsletters and occasional personal notes. Any time a partner tries to reach me on the telephone, they get through to me directly. I value and respect my partners. I recognize their vital contribution to the ministry that God has called me to.

Once a year, I ask our partners to mail me their most critical prayer request needs. I spend an entire day in prayer and fasting, praying over every need individually, calling them out to the Lord. In addition to this, I pray for my partners on a regular basis in my private secret place. If one of my partners goes into the hospital or has a family tragedy and I am physically able to visit, I do so.

If you want a long-term relationship with your partners, never view the relationship as simply "they give to me." You must, in turn, give your time, ministry, and prayers to them. It truly is a partnership if both parties give of themselves for God's greater calling.

Your ministry success is determined by relationships. Relationships from God are as crucial to your ministry survival as air is to your body.

We are to be responsible stewards of our relationships. Take care of the names and addresses that God gives you or you don't qualify for any more. You are responsible for maintaining the kingdom connections that God has established in your life.

If an individual gives you their address and/or phone number, record it and file it. I cannot tell you how many people God brought into my life in my early days as an evangelist, and because of a failure on my part to file their information, I lost access to their lives and the blessing they wanted to be to my ministry.

When individuals express an interest in your ministry by purchasing something from your table, they are saying that they are interested in your life and what you are doing. These are individuals with whom you will want to stay in contact. Write them and let them know when you have new ministry products they might be interested in.

Let them know of other ministry projects that you are involved in and exchange prayer requests with them. When they have asked permission to be in your life, then you have a right and an obligation to pursue that relationship. I recommend that an evangelist correspond with those on his mailing list on a monthly basis. Your ministry letter should arrive in their home by the first of every month.

By cultivating the three areas of ministry revenue described in this chapter, you will build a productive ministry that not only provides for the needs of your household, but also enables you to fulfill the call of God on your life and walk through every open door He makes available for you.

CHAPTER EIGHT

Writing Your First Book

Every evangelist should write books.
A book is your presence somewhere else.
A book never compromises.
A book never argues.
A book is never intimidated.

A book can go places you can't and reach people that you can't reach. It will stay in places where you can't stay. You may give one of your books to one individual, but ten people may read the same copy. It *multiplies* your ministry.

Somebody needs what you have or God wouldn't have given it to you. You must be a good steward of that and sow it to somebody else. Every evangelist can write his own books. It doesn't matter what your educational training or ability is.

Reasons why some will never write a book:

1. "I don't have enough education."
2. "I don't have enough money."
3. "I don't know how to write a book."
4. "Nobody would ever read it."
5. "I don't have enough time."

Time is in short supply for every evangelist, but a wise evangelist will structure his time for the things that are most important. John Wesley understood the value of a book. In his lifetime, he wrote hundreds of books. Billy Graham has written numerous books. "For God so loved the world that He gave His only begotten Son." As one preacher says, God sent his Son, but He left His Book."

How to Write Your First Book

Oral Roberts was once speaking to a young man about writing his first 160-page book. The young man responded that he couldn't write a 160-page book. Brother Roberts asked him if he could write a ten-page letter, and the young man replied, "Sure." Oral Roberts said, "Then write one sixteen times."

An evangelist should write at least a thirty-two-page book on his particular theme or focus. If your focus is on family ministry, then write a book on the family. If your focus is on souls, then write a book on soul-winning. If your focus is on marriage, then write a book on marriage. If your focus is on revival, then write a book on revival. If your focus is music, then write a book on music. Whatever your main ministry focus is, you should be able to at least write a thirty-two-page book on it and make it available.

Every evangelist should write a discipleship booklet that he can give to those who are saved under his ministry. It should highlight all of the basics that a new convert should understand – water baptism, church attendance, what kind of church to look for, Bible reading, prayer, the Holy Spirit, tithing, finding his own ministry/assignment, growth, understanding the cross and the victory over sin, etc.

Numerous times in scripture, God told his preachers to *write down* what he gave them. See Exodus 17:14, 34:17; Nehemiah 9:

38; Isaiah 30:8; Jeremiah 30:2; Ezekiel 43:11; Habakkuk 2:2; Acts 15:20.

Remember a book is your legacy – your life on paper. A soul-winning evangelist will take advantage of this.

CHAPTER NINE

Ministry Banquet

A time for victory reports and vision casting!

Every evangelist should have an annual ministry banquet. A banquet is your opportunity to have friends, partners, and family gather to hear victory reports of your past year and hear your visions and goals for the upcoming year.

A banquet can be held in a church fellowship hall, hotel, or local business conference room. To develop a tradition, the banquet should be held once a year in the same month You should begin at 7:00 p.m., and conclude no later than 9:00 p.m.

8 Steps To Preparing for Your Banquet

To achieve maximum results, preparation and planning for your banquet should be done months in advance.

1. Prepare a Banquet Budget.
Obtain four different quotes for every item of purchase involving your banquet. Don't be afraid to negotiate. Inform those you are getting quotes from that your banquet will be held every year, and

you are looking for someone to do business with long-term.

2. Make a list of those you want to invite.

This should obviously include *everyone* on your mailing list within the same state. Never assume certain individuals would not attend your banquet. I never make people's decision for them. We have had people drive as far as six hours to attend our banquets.

Send invitations to all of the people on your mailing list within your home state, or within a six-hour, one-way driving distance. Your list should include family, people you do business with (doctors, bankers, printers, post office employees, etc.), people that you frequently come in contact with, people to whom you would feel comfortable sending a Christmas card. The list should include the same groups of individuals in your spouse's circle of influence. Hundreds of names can easily be gathered.

3. Book the time, date, and location of your banquet.

Be sensitive regarding the date for your banquet so that it doesn't conflict with major events such as holidays or activities in your city. If your primary attendance is going to come from a few key churches in your area, then call their secretaries months in advance and confirm if they have a conflicting event on the day of your banquet. Prior commitments may keep people who would normally want to attend from attending your banquet. The best nights for the banquet are Friday or Saturday, with Friday being the best choice. Avoid nights of heavy public interest or seasonal times of the year such as football season or the opening night of hunting season, etc.

4. Print post cards inviting people to your banquet.

These post cards will serve as an announcement that your "official invitation" is coming soon. Our post cards simply say something to this effect:

> *"Watch your mail in the next few days for your official invitation
> to the Worldreach Ministries Annual Celebration Dinner to be
> held at (time, date, location etc.)"*

This post card contains the same information as the invitation, but puts those you're inviting on alert to watch for the official invitation, which will contain their RSVP. Your post cards should be mailed approximately six to eight weeks before your banquet. Seven days after mailing the post cards, you should mail the official invitation.

5. Develop and print quality invitations.

Print quality invitations and envelopes. You don't have to spend a lot of money, but make them look professional and have them printed and done with a spirit of excellence. They should briefly detail the location, date and time of your banquet and what will take place. We typically state on our invitations that it will be a night of ministry, reports from the past year, special music, and a video presentation. If time and money permit, you may decorate the room with the theme and focus of your ministry.

Typically, we invite a greater number of individuals to our banquets then we have on our mailing list. I encourage you to do the same. Your envelope should include an RSVP return slip stating how many people will be in their party. The return slip should have a place for them to put their name, address and telephone number. Also, it should have a small disclaimer that says "Adults Only Please." Your banquet should be adults only for the purpose of keeping an atmosphere of seriousness while you share your vision. There is nothing as frustrating as having a child interrupt the most important financial night of the year. It's your banquet. You deserve to be heard. Plan in advance against any distractions that will shift people's focus away from your words.

This is your one big night of the year. Make it count for God. Make it count for your ministry. Make it count for your family.

Our first ministry banquet had thirty-five in attendance. We used the fellowship hall of a local church and brought the food in. Today we find holding our banquets in a hotel allows our ministry to attract people from various denominations.

Each table should have one pen per person, with an envelope and form to fill out, indicating their level of support.

6. Maintain a list of those who RSVP and mail them a confirmation letter.

The confirmation letter should say something like: "We have received your RSVP. ___ number of seats have been reserved in your name etc. We look forward to seeing you there."

7. Approximately ten to twelve days prior to the banquet date, call everyone on your list.

Call those you haven't heard from and inform them the banquet wouldn't be the same without them. Ask them if you can count on their attendance.

8. Remember that five to ten percent of those who RSVP will not attend, so keep this in mind when preparing the meals.

Conducting Your Banquet

Your banquet should include a time of eating and fellowship, followed by a brief victory report from the past year. You may want to show a video or slide show or bring in someone who has been saved in your ministry to give a brief testimony.

You may want to have a display of pictures of places that you've gone or crusades that you've done overseas. Share your vision for the next year, then close the night by telling them that there are four ways they can partner with you.

1. They can be your prayer partners. Briefly share your belief in the power of prayer and your ministry's need for intercessors.

2. They can become monthly partners. Share the need for partners who will stand with you financially each month.

3. They can sow a generous offering that night. Many individuals will be excited to partner with your vision and have the ability to sow a generous offering. In addition, invite those in your audience who own their own business to sow a large seed representing their business.

4. If they are already a monthly partner, they can increase their pledge over the next year.

Ask those who have partnered with you for a year or more to consider increasing their giving amount each month.

After you have finished sharing the above opportunities, ask the audience to take the response card on their table and bow with you for prayer. Instruct the people to ask the Holy Spirit to speak to them as to what they should give. When you are finished leading them in prayer, have them complete the card and place it in the envelope you have provided.

This will be the conclusion of your banquet and should end

with a joyful atmosphere of thanks to God for the work that is going to be accomplished over the next twelve months. *Never* keep people past 9:00 p.m.

You may want to have a table in the lobby with your ministry products on it. At the conclusion of your banquet (after you have received your offering), announce that everything on your table is discounted by two-thirds as an additional way of saying thanks for their attendance and partnership.

An annual banquet is a fantastic way to launch your ministry to new heights and to celebrate face to face with those who are helping to make your ministry happen. It's an opportunity for you to show people that you love them, to pray for them, and for them to pray for you. A wise 21st century evangelist will plan a successful ministry banquet every year for the rest of his ministry.

CHAPTER TEN

Habits of Successful Evangelists

Habit will take you further than desire.

What you do habitually is the real you. What you do occasionally is the potential you. Discipline births habits and habits birth success.

Merely wanting to be a good evangelist does not make you a good evangelist. Loving Jesus does not make you a fruitful and successful evangelist. Having a passion for the lost does not guarantee that you will reach the lost. You must have a plan.

17 Habits Of Highly Successful Evangelists

1. They have a prayer life.

Leonard Ravenhill said, "No man is greater than his prayer life. The secret of praying is praying in secret."

Pastor Jim Morris, my spiritual father for more than a decade, told me the first weekend I met him, "If you are not a man of discipline, you will never be a man of God"

Your prayer life cannot be underestimated. It is only to the degree that you give yourself to God, that He, in turn, can give Himself *through you* to others.

Dr. W.E. Sangster said, "How shall I feel at the judgment if multitudes of missed opportunities pass before me in full review and all my excuses prove to be disguises of my cowardess and pride."

It is recorded in scripture on more than one occasion that Jesus spent whole nights in prayer to the Father. John Wesley rose at four o'clock each morning to begin his day in prayer.

Study the lives of great men of God and you will find that all of them had a disciplined prayer life, and those who didn't rise in the middle of the night to pray rose early in the morning. Leonard Ravenhill always said, "No man is greater than his prayer life." In this generation of technology and new inventions, internet sermons, and numerous other study tools, there is still no substitute in the life of the evangelist for intimate time with God.

No evangelist will ever properly thunder in Pharaoh's court until he has first taken his shoes off with God at the burning bush.

2. They read the word of God.

Never develop the habit of merely reading the Bible in an attempt to find sermon material. Read the word of God because you love it (Psalm 119:165). Read the word of God because it changes you. Read the word of God because it cleanses you (Psalm 119:9). Read the word of God to know God (Psalm 119:10). Read the word of God to know the will of God for your life.

3. They listen to the Word of God on cassette tape.

Listening is different from reading. Romans 10:17 says *"Faith cometh by hearing, and hearing by the word of God."*

4. They pray in the Holy Spirit. (see Jude 1:20)

5. They have numerous mentors.
An evangelist should have several mentors, but one main spiritual father. Take advantage of the discoveries of others.

6. They have written goals.
Only three percent of the earth's population have written goals. It has been said that three percent of the world owns more than the other ninety-seven percent combined. Written goals are a must to the evangelist.

7. They continually develop ministry tools and resources that equip the body of Christ to reach the lost.

8. They have a circle of counsel.
Proverbs 24:6b says, *"And in a multitude of counsel there is safety."*

9. They value and respect their time (Psalm 89:47).
If you don't respect and manage your time, you don't have a future in the ministry.

10. They have a pattern of fasting (see Matthew 6:16).

11. They continually read.
Note Paul's request of Timothy for his upcoming visit with Paul in prison. II Tim. 4:13. says, *"The cloak that I left at Troas with Carpus, when thou comest, bring with thee, and the books..."*

12. They pay attention to the needs of their family.
A foolish evangelist gives his full attention to saving the families of

the world while neglecting to reach his own.

13. They are sensitive and obedient to the protocol of the church they are preaching in.

14. They never betray the trust of a senior pastor.

You will find in your ministry the Holy Spirit will lead you to some churches, not for the people in the church but to minister to the pastor of that congregation.

Many pastors feel they have no one in their congregation to talk to. Preachers need to talk to preachers. Shepherds don't talk well to sheep. Sheep don't talk well to shepherds. It is imperative for you as an evangelist to develop the reputation that pastors can share their burdens, their victories, and their concerns with you and you won't share those with anyone.

15. They constantly learn and share fresh ideas with pastors.

Traveling as an evangelist will expose you to the best and worst of ministry. Become a student of what works and what doesn't. When asked by pastors for your advice on local church issues, be ready to give a practical, relevant answer.

16. They are very aware of the difficulties pastors face.

Become familiar with the day-to-day struggles and challenges a pastor encounters.

17. They function out of a home church.

There is nothing more alarming than an evangelist who preaches everywhere, but reports and submits to no one. Continually update your pastor on your ministry's progress and goals.

CHAPTER ELEVEN

The Preaching of an Evangelist

New Testament preaching is always law to the proud and grace to the humble.

———

The tragedy of modern preaching is that grace is given to everyone. Jesus never did that.

The great Puritan preachers of the 17th and 18th centuries understood the New Testament pattern for preaching.

Consider the following statements made by John Wesley and Charles Spurgeon:

"Before I can preach love, mercy, and grace, I must preach sin, Law and judgment."

– John Wesley

"Lower the law, and you dim the light by which man perceives his guilt; this is a very serious loss to the sinner rather than a gain; for it lessens the likelihood of his conviction and

conversion. I say you have deprived the Gospel of its ablest auxiliary (its most powerful weapon). When you have set aside the law, you have taken away from it the schoolmaster that is to bring men to Christ.

They will never accept grace until they tremble before a just and holy law. Therefore the law serves a most necessary purpose, and it must not be removed from its place. I do not believe that any man can preach the Gospel who does not preach the law."

– Charles Spurgeon

The following scriptures give us an indication of how Jesus dealt with people using the principle, "Law to the proud, grace to the humble."

In Luke chapter 18, Jesus sent a rich young ruler away by giving him law. Examine the text. The young man asked Jesus how to inherit eternal life. Sounds like a great question, but Jesus knew the man had money as his "god," thereby breaking the first commandment of having *"no other gods before me."*

When you have another god before the Lord, you are worshipping that "god" which breaks the second commandment of having *"no graven image nor bowing down to worship it."* When you have a false god in your life, and God does not have first place, then you are worshipping a false god and are an idolater.

If you are an idolater and claim to be right with God, then you break the third commandment by taking the name of the Lord that you represent in vain.

Then when you go to church, you cannot remember the Sabbath day and keep it holy because you come into God's house as an idolater. If you were a young Jewish boy and you were raised to be a good Jew, but yet you become an idolater, you've *"dishonored your father and mother."*

You have stolen your life, time, and possessions from God by using them on yourself and you have coveted money.

So Jesus gave the young man the law by telling him that he was lacking one thing and he needed to sell everything that he had and give it to the poor. The young man was "very sorrowful" and went away. Jesus did not go after him. Jesus gave him law, not grace, because the young man was proud and not humble.

On another occasion in Luke, Chapter 10, we have a self-professing teacher of God's law who asked how to be right with God

Jesus asked him what was written in the law and the man answered, *"Thou shalt love the Lord thy God with all thy heart, and with all thy soul, and with all thy strength, and with all thy mind; and thy neighbor as thyself."* Jesus responded, *"Thou hast answered right: this do, and thou shalt live."* The Bible tells us that the man was "willing to justify himself," and asked *"Who is my neighbor?"* This clearly demonstrates the man's pride. Jesus did not give the man grace, but rebuked and exposed him for being a law-breaker by telling the parable of the Samaritan.

In John, Chapter 3, Nicodemus came humbly to Jesus at night acknowledging that Jesus came from God. Jesus did not give him law. He gave him grace and told him that he needed to be born again.

The woman caught in adultery deserved the wrath of the law, but her humility in the presence of Jesus allowed His grace to be given to her. *"Neither do I condemn you. Go and sin no more."*

3 Golden Rules For Speaking In Churches

1. Obey the pastor's instruction.

If a pastor tells you to be finished at twelve o'clock, don't preach five minutes past that. Don't preach one minute past that. Obey the protocol of the house. Numerous evangelists are never invited back to a church, not because they weren't anointed or because the people didn't like them, but they simply did not obey the instructions of the pastor. When you are in a man's pulpit, he is your authority, so adapt to the wishes of the house.

2. Always say something to build up the pastor from the pulpit.

Remember that the pastor is your door to that congregation. Very few churches around the world understand how blessed they are to have the pastor they have. When you see a pastor week after week, you begin to get used to him. It is the rare congregation that totally grasps the quality and caliber of the man that they have in their pulpit.

As an evangelist, always thank the pastor in front of the people for the privilege of being there and praise his uniqueness. If he's a good administrator, say so. If he's a great preacher, publicly acknowledge that. If all he talks about is missions when you're around him, then celebrate the fact that he has a heart for the Great Commission. Say something from the pulpit that reminds those people of how blessed they are to have that individual as their pastor.

3. Never preach against the main doctrine of the church that you are speaking in.

If you're invited to speak in a Baptist church, don't speak on "Ten Reasons Why We Should Speak in Tongues." If you are in a Church of Christ church, don't speak on "Ten Reasons Why We Should Have Musical Instruments." You're not there to change the doctrine of that church. You may disagree with it and God may disagree with it, but it isn't your job to change it. I am speaking here of "non-salvation" doctrines.

Observe the style of the church that you are preaching in. If you're in a small country church where they are accustomed to old-fashioned, Holy Ghost, "screaming at the top of your lungs" preaching, then it would probably not be advantageous to speak quietly in a monotone like Mr. Rogers. At the same time, if you are in a sensitive church that is used to the pastor "teaching" from a stool with a cup of coffee in his hand, you will blow the people away if you come and preach at the top of your lungs. So adapt your style while retaining your own uniqueness. Don't try to be someone else's preacher. You can be yourself, but at the same time be wise to your listening audience so that they will receive the word of the Lord. A wise preacher once said, "I don't want to put a fork in their eye when I'm trying to put food in their mouth."

Preaching With Microphones

Learn to preach with different microphones. Learn to be comfortable wearing a lapel microphone so that your hands are free. Learn to become comfortable preaching with a hand-held microphone with your hands not as free. It is the author's opinion that preaching with a cordless, hand-held microphone is the best method for preserving your voice over a long period of time.

The Evangelist's Voice

The evangelist has only one voice to use for God in his lifetime. Many evangelists have abused their voices only to regret it in later years when they didn't have a professional voice left to speak with.

There is nothing more disheartening than to see a man of God with a fire in his heart, but no vocal chord strength to communicate his message.

Every athlete knows that if he wants to compete for the long term, he has to care for his body. People would laugh at a football player who never went to practice. People would mock a boxer who never worked out. But almost no one understands the importance of warming up your voice before you speak. *Your voice is the tool of your trade.*

No matter how close to God you are, no matter how much revelation God has given you, you cannot communicate orally without a voice. A wise evangelist will study and learn principles of voice control, pitch, tone, and pace. These are important. I regret the times in my life when I have raised my voice too often for the sake of sounding anointed, only to find that my voice was not what it needed to be a few days later.

You may want to consult a doctor in your area who is a throat or voice specialist. Have a checkup at the beginning of your ministry. It would be wise to obtain some advice and exercises on how to strengthen the voice and the vocal chords. Each person's voice has a natural tone, pitch, and vocal range ability.

Learning about and understanding your voice is as crucial to the longevity of your ministry as prayer and obedience are to your anointing.

Crucial Habits for Maintaining a Healthy Voice:

1. Never drink ice water before, during, or immediately after you preach.

Imagine you've just come in from a hot day outdoors only to have someone throw a bucket of ice water on your back. You would instantly react and arch back. This is what your vocal chords do when you preach a sermon, get hot, and then pour ice water on them. Though you don't feel it, they are reacting.

Always ask those who are serving your water during ministry times to bring water that is lukewarm or at room temperature. Warm your voice up before you preach. For some vocal exercises that can be done in the shower, car, or during the song service, consult a local voice coach or a throat doctor. Remember you are a lifetime vocal athlete.

Treat your voice with respect. Your speaking ministry depends on it.

2. Learn to use the microphone to your advantage.

It is my personal opinion that the best microphone you can preach with is a cordless hand-held. A microphone in your hand allows you to control how close the microphone is to your mouth. A lapel or tie-mic does not. It stays where it is clipped. The author understands that you will raise your voice as you preach, but you can use the microphone and the sound system to raise your voice within a range that you are capable of reaching. Every listener can tell when a speaker is trying to take his voice somewhere it is not capable of going. Understand your range.

3. Minimize the amount of singing that you do before you preach.

If your ministry involves singing, you will function differently. However, if your ministry is the ministry of preaching only, don't wear your voice out singing for an hour and a half and then try to preach. Everybody else quits singing and sits down while you continue speaking. So if you preach for forty-five minutes and sing forty-five minutes prior to that, you have used your voice non-stop in a strenuous way for an hour and a half. Multiply this over the course of a year, and you will see how you put unnecessary wear on your voice. You can sing and feel free to worship the Lord with the congregation, but realize that the pastor didn't call you there to sing praise and worship songs. He called you there to preach. So sing lightly, whisper, or even lip-sync. There's nothing wrong with this. You can still express a heart of worship and adoration to the Lord by merely conserving your voice. No Olympic sprinter runs from the hotel to the stadium before beginning a race. Likewise, an evangelist needs to understand that to be a good steward of the voice God has given him, he must preserve it for what God has called him to do with it – preach.

Four Lessons on the Altar Call

Every evangelist should make an altar call.

1. The altar call is Biblical.

An altar call is nothing more than a public call to make a decision for Jesus Christ. Jesus called people publicly, "Zachaeus, come down from the tree. Let's go to your house." "Matthew, get up from the table and follow me." He called the disciples of John the Baptist and gave them a public invitation to follow Him. John the Baptist baptized in public, "Repent, for the kingdom of God is at hand."

2. Give an altar call in every service.

Never make people's decisions for them. Never assume that a lost person is not listening to your message.

I recently attended a minister's conference that was by invitation only for those in the ministry, and I witnessed more than one person responding to an altar call for salvation! With your cassette tapes and messages being sent out, you need to have an altar call in every service, no matter what you're preaching on.

3. Never allow the sound man to stop recording your services just because you're making an altar call.

This does not mean that the tape has to continue to run endlessly and record people crying or expressing emotion. But the actual instructions that the evangelist gives regarding how to be saved and how to pray do need to be included on the tape, so that if someone is listening to it two years from now, they will hear those instructions and know how to respond. For this reason and others, always have your sermons taped.

4. Never assume that people know how to get right with God. They need to be walked through the process.

After you've led people to Christ, in every altar call, *always* pray for the sick. This doesn't mean that you have to lay hands on everyone in the audience. However, do simply tell people that not only is Jesus Christ a Savior, but He's also a healer. Ask them to put their hand on the part of their body where they're sick and pray the prayer of faith over them. Always pray in the name of Jesus Christ of Nazareth, by whose stripes you were healed. Always pray for people's assignment. After you've prayed for salvation and for the sick, ask individuals to lay hands on their forehead, and pray aloud that the Holy Spirit will reveal their assignment or calling for their life. Always have some follow up material for those who are saved.

An altar call should be given at every service and the altar call can be presented differently and done at different times in the service.

The New Testament evangelist opens the door of the Gospel to sinners in every service.

CHAPTER TWELVE

The Evangelist and His Family

The first institution that God ever created.

———

God created the family before He created the church. Being a full-time evangelist can be very straining on an evangelist's family. My personal opinion is that it is not healthy or practical for an evangelist to stay away from home for extended periods of time without taking his family with him.

Four Practical Suggestions for the Family that Travels Together

1. Insist on quality accommodations.

Most pastors are very considerate about this. If you feel unsafe or unsettled in a particular situation, kindly share that with the pastor. If your wife is uneasy about a place you've been asked to stay, request a change. Information about your lodging requirements should be sent to a church weeks or months before you arrive. You should state the type of room you prefer (upstairs, downstairs, non-smoking etc.). If you're uncomfortable staying in someone's home, don't be afraid to share that with the pastor.

When staying in a motel, allow your wife to decorate the room with her own creativity. Candles or framed pictures of loved ones you are carrying with you and momentos from home can be placed around the room. This gives the room a more pleasant atmosphere when traveling with your family.

However, motel rooms can be depressing. Stay out of them as much as possible. Take work you have brought to the local library. This will provide the quiet atmosphere that you need without the depression or distractions of a motel room.

If you're traveling in a motor home or RV, treat it as your home. Don't allow the church members, deacons, or youth group to just randomly invade your "home." Your wife and children need a sense of privacy and security.

While you may go to a different church each week and your RV may be "new to them," it is still your home. Insist upon this privacy, and don't allow anyone into your home uninvited.

Home Base

Every evangelist needs a home base and every evangelist should have a home. It is my opinion that the advantages of having a home or an apartment that is yours far outweigh the disadvantages. To have a place to come home to, no matter how long you have been gone, provides security, comfort, and privacy.

Have a bank, print shop, post office, or small-town airport that you do business with continually. If you are in a large city, develop long-term relationships with the people with whom you do business. You need a home base where people know who you are and know what you're about.

2. Don't feel pressured that your family has to attend each service that you preach in a revival.

If this is an issue with the senior pastor, merely inform him that your family travels with you continually, and that for their own rest and privacy, they do not attend church with you every evening. The pastor has asked you to come and preach, and they will be there with you most of the time. Courteously remind the pastor that you speak somewhere several times each week and your family, like his, is not expected to go to church 185 days of the year.

3. Don't pressure your wife or children to involve themselves in ministry they're not comfortable with.

The pastor has invited you to come. If your wife or children are not comfortable playing musical instruments or singing, they should not be pressured to do so.

4. Don't discuss negative church business or issues in front of your children.

Keep your conversations about the pastors you preach for and the churches you preach in positive and God-honoring. Never allow your children to sense that you are unhappy with a particular pastor or his congregation. Never allow your children to hear you express anger or hurt concerning your perceived wrong treatment by a pastor, especially in the area of finances.

Traveling Alone When Married

There are many ways that a wife can show support for her husband when he is on the road and she is not with him. Here are just a few suggestions:

1. When he calls home, Mom should allow the children to talk to Dad on the telephone. Many times, because children are in their home environment and have their friends and mother around, they don't miss the father as much as he misses them. It's very important that the children be taught to respect their father's emotions and to respect him as the man of God in their house. So when Dad calls while on the road, they will drop what they're doing and talk to him with a joyful attitude. The wife should not allow the children to give the evangelist the impression that speaking to him when he calls is a burden to them. A wise wife will continually speak well of her husband's ministry while he is gone.

Include the children in the ministry. Continually communicate to your children that they are your best partners. In God's eyes, they are as much a part of the ministry as their daddy.

Many times I have returned home from a trip, pulled my sons close and excitedly proclaimed how many souls *we saw* come to Christ this week.

2. A wife can keep unnecessary news items from her husband before his ministry time. She should not call him at his motel room twenty minutes before he is going to preach to five hundred people and tell him that a pipe has burst and the bedroom has flooded. Bad news that an evangelist is unable to correct while on the road can create frustration, depression, homesickness and loneliness and minimize his ministry effectiveness.

3. A wife should communicate to her husband that she is praying for him. When he calls, she should tell him that she has been praying for his meetings and she should ask specific questions such as, "How many are being saved, healed, baptized in the Holy Spirit and called to preach?" These types of questions show her

husband that she is genuinely interested.

A wife's first question to her husband should not be, "How much was the offering?" This totally puts the focus and the pressure on the finances and the focus should be on the ministry and what was accomplished for God.

The Single Evangelist

The single evangelist will face the same temptations that a married evangelist will face when traveling alone. The difference, of course, is that one goes home at the end of a meeting to a wife and family, while the single evangelist will remain alone. There are definite advantages to being a single evangelist, such as the ability to stay gone for extended periods of time without inconveniencing other family members. The personal costs are less for a single evangelist than for a married evangelist. However, there are disadvantages as well, such as loneliness. It is important for both the married and single evangelists to realize that their reputation can be tarnished and damaged by the people they are seen to associate with.

Remember, Jesus sent His disciples out two by two. Every evangelist should immediately seek the Lord for a traveling companion. This will provide companionship, accountability, and protection.

When a single evangelist begins a relationship with someone who could become a potential spouse, it is important that they submit themselves to Godly counsel regarding marriage possibilities.

Many young evangelists believe that all their wife needs to do is be someone who loves to travel. This, in my opinion, is not the main consideration for a young man when seeking a wife. The other side of the issue is not whether your future wife will travel with you, but will she allow you to travel when she cannot go herself.

Packing Properly

There is an art to packing. Understanding how to pack, when to pack, and what to pack will make you a more effective evangelist. There are many excellent books on the subject. Check with your local library or book store.

Luggage

1. Every evangelist needs good luggage. Never buy any luggage without wheels on it.

2. Negotiate everything. If you're at a specialty store, ask for a corporate discount, which is normally 40% off. You have not because you ask not. If possible, your luggage should be non-traditional colors so that it is easy to spot at an airport. You also lower the risk of someone else mistaking your luggage for theirs and picking it up.

3. Keep a supply of toiletries in your suitcase that you never unpack. Then when you leave, all you have to do is pack your clothes. This habit will eliminate trying to remember to repack toiletries over and over.

4. In addition to luggage, you may want to invest in an attractive attaché case to carry to the pulpit. You shouldn't be afraid to spend some money on this. It should be handsome and something you feel comfortable carrying your work in.

CHAPTER THIRTEEN

The Evangelist and Discouragement

Discouragement can be disabling.
Discouragement can be deadly.

Every evangelist will experience discouragement. All great evangelists of past generations have been discouraged.

Elijah, the prophet, was so discouraged that he asked God to take him home. The biographies of great men of God reveal that each of them had days or seasons of discouragement. How you respond to discouragement will determine your next level of success, usefulness, and greatness.

Remember, it is only to the degree that you give yourself to God that He, in turn, can give Himself, through you, to others.

Eleven Keys to Handling Discouragement

1. Despise not the day of small beginnings (2 Timothy 4:12; Zachariah 4:10)

It takes time to build a ministry. Great ministries are not birthed in a week. Refuse to allow frustration and discouragement to handicap your ministry. Remind yourself continually that God is moving you forward. There will be times of rejection *throughout* your ministry.

2. Understand that everyone experiences discouragement.

Jesus was rejected by the Saducees and Pharisees. Jesus said in the scripture that He couldn't do miracles in his home town because of their unbelief. He also said a prophet is without honor in his home country. Thousands of people walked past Jesus and never accepted who He was. They totally rejected Him as the Messiah. He experienced temporal rejection when His father turned His face and blackened the sky, causing Him to cry out, "My God, my God, why have you forsaken me?" Every great man or woman of God experiences rejection.

3. Recognize that discouragement is for your good.

The Bible says in Romans 8:28 that *"...all things work to together for good to them that love God, to them who are the called according to His purpose."* Every day of your life, God is building you, molding you, making you. He is the vine and you are the branches. *"...walk in the spirit, and ye shall not fulfill the lust of the flesh"* (Galatians 5:16).

4. Discouragement is temporal.

In moments of fatigue, one act of rejection can turn your thinking into the wrong mindset where you believe no one wants your ministry. Recognize that rejection comes only for a limited time and it's never as great as it seems.

5. During times of discouragement, obey Philippians 4:8.

"Think on things that are true, honest, just, lovely, holy, pure..."

6. Evaluate the reasons for your rejection.

Ask yourself some tough questions. Was I rejected because of something that I did wrong? Was I rejected because my spirit wasn't right? Was I rejected because I conveyed arrogance and pride? If you answer "yes" to these questions, ask the Lord to forgive you and go and seek the forgiveness of others if necessary. If the answer to the above questions is "no," then be at peace with God and yourself. You are now in the same position as the apostles, the church fathers, and all great evangelists, past, present, and future.

I can think of some churches where I have preached and done the very best that I could. We had people saved, the Holy Spirit moved in the services, and the people responded with favor to our ministry. I had good fellowship with the pastor, and yet for some reason, he never invited me back. You must never allow this type of rejection to put a damper on your entire ministry. Some ministers would not invite the Apostle Paul back for a second time. Other times, evangelists are not invited back because of something they did that offended the pastor, and he is uncomfortable sharing that. In either case, keep a clean conscience before God and man and go full speed ahead.

7. Put all things behind you.

"...But this one thing I do, forgetting those things which are behind, and reaching forth unto those things which are before, I press toward the mark for the prize of the high calling of God in Christ Jesus" (Phil. 3:13a-14). Putting all things behind us means successes and failures. If we dwell on our success, pride enters in. If we dwell on our failures, we are overwhelmed. Evangelist George Whitfield once said, "I was honored today to have had a few stones, dirt, rotten eggs, and pieces of dead cats thrown at me."

8. Learn to celebrate small victories.

In your early days as an evangelist, there will be days of discouragement and days of encouragement. Every new milestone should be celebrated while you're planning for the next accomplishment. Take time to remember what God has done.

Numerous times in scripture, God told Moses to remind the children of Israel of the miracles of the Lord. This was to keep past victories in front of the people.

Many pastors on Sunday mornings sit on their platforms and become discouraged before they even preach. They look out to see who didn't show up, who is late, and who is not smiling. Instead of celebrating who is there and what is about to take place, they allow disappointment to become discouragement! *"For as he thinketh in his heart, so is he..."(Proverbs 23:7)*. The Holy Spirit told us what to think about in Philippians 4:8, *"Finally, brethren, whatsoever things are true, whatsoever things are honest, whatsoever things are just, whatsoever things are pure, whatsoever things are lovely, whatsoever things are of good report; if there be any virtue, and if there be any praise, think on these things."* Remember, what you are thankful for is what God brings you more of.

9. Document each new ministry milestone.

Don't trust your mind to remember victories. You will want to remember your early days and the doors that God opened for you.

One of the regrets of my early ministry was not keeping a journal as God performed financial and other miracles. Years later, it is more difficult to remember the details. When God does something for you, it is worth documenting for yourself and for your future. Today I document the victories as I go along, and I am leaving them for my children and my children's children to see the heritage of God's answering of our prayers and showing Himself strong on our behalf.

10. Save testimony letters.

People that are saved, healed and delivered under your ministry may write you to let you know that your ministry has made a difference in their lives and thanking you for being used of God to touch their lives.

File these and on days when you are feeling discouraged, they will be a source of encouragement to remind you how God has used you in the past, and how He is going to use you in the future. It may be helpful to post these on a wall so you will constantly see them.

11. Write down your goals.

Give God opportunities to show Himself strong on your behalf. If you are asking God for a certain number of monthly partners or a certain number of bookings in one year, write these figures down. Pray for them and ask for them. Document as God begins to answer them. Answers to prayer will motivate and encourage you.

CHAPTER FOURTEEN

The Reward of the Evangelist

"Take heed to the ministry which thou hast received in the Lord that thou fulfill it." (Galatians 4:17)

The Bible promises a crown of life to the one who has been faithful. The apostle Paul told Timothy, "I have fought a good fight. I have finished my course. I have kept the faith."

An evangelist will have many rewards given to him for his service to the Lord. There will be souls saved, bodies healed, and people called to preach under your ministry. As you sow into people's lives, you will reap a harvest in years to come by seeing God raise up those your ministry has touched and thrust them into their assignment.

The greatest reward that an evangelist will ever receive will be on that great and final day when he sees Jesus face to face and hears the words, "Well done, good and faithful servant..."

God has called you to be a part of the 21st century harvest!

It is an accelerated harvest fulfilling the prophecy of Amos 12.

These are the greatest days in church history, so lift up your eyes and look on the field. Fix your eyes on Jesus and "make full proof of your ministry."

The harvest is waiting... *go and bring it in!*

WOULD GOD CALL YOU A CHRISTIAN?

The word "Christian" is perhaps the most misused word in the English language. Many people consider themselves to be Christians and yet have no idea what the word means, involves, or implies. Simply assuming that one is a Christian is not safe because it is possible to be both sincere and wrong.

The Bible shows us what a Christian's life will look like, so it makes sense to see if the One who authored the Bible would call us Christians. Please honestly examine yourself by answering the following questions. I John 5:13 says, *"I write these things that you may know you have eternal life."*

1. Do you claim to be a Christian but live in intentional sin?

"If we say that we have fellowship with Him, and walk in darkness, we lie, and do not the truth" (I John 1:16).

2. Do you keep God's commandments?

"And hereby we do know that we know Him, if we keep His commandments. He that saith, I know Him and keepeth not His commandments is a liar,

and the truth is not in him" (I John 2:3,4).

3. Do you hate anyone?

"He that saith he is in the light, and hateth his brother, is in darkness even until now. If a man say, I love God, and hateth his brother, he is a liar: for he that loveth not his brother whom he has seen, how can he love God whom he hath not seen?" (I John 2:9, 4:20).

4. Do you love this world and the "things" that are in the world?

"Love not the world, neither the things that are in the world. If any man love the world, the love of the Father is not in him" (I John 4:15).

5. If you have heard the Gospel before, have you always lived for God? Or have you always done the things that you know are right?

"Let that therefore abide in you, which ye have heard from the beginning. If that which ye have heard from the beginning shall remain in you, ye shall continue in the Son, and in the Father" (I John 2:24).

Did you answer "yes" to one or more of these questions? Perhaps you're still unsure. Let's look at another "mirror" that God has placed for us in His word: the Ten Commandments. Answer "yes" or "no" to these:

1. Has God always been first in your life?
2. Have you ever shaped a god to suit your beliefs?
3. Have you ever taken God's name in vain?
4. Have you always gone to church and kept the Sabbath holy?
5. Have you always honored your father and mother?
6. Have you ever murdered? (The Bible says hatred is the same

as murder.)

7. Have you ever committed adultery? (The Bible says lust of the heart is the same thing.)

8. Have you ever stolen?

9. Have you ever lied?

10. Have you ever coveted (desired) what belongs to someone else?

As we can see, the God of the Bible demands a much higher standard than man. James 2:10 says, *"For whosoever shall keep the whole law, and yet offend in one point, he is guilty of all."*

The God of Scripture takes the word "Christian" very seriously. Merely claiming oneself to be a Christian doesn't make it so any more than going to a supermarket makes someone a bag of groceries. The Bible tells us in Hebrews 9:27, *"And as it is appointed unto men once to die, but after this the judgment."* This means that you will stand before God one day and only what He says about your life will matter.

We Can Be Sure

Because God loves us and desired to save us from the consequences of our disobedience (eternal Hell), Jesus Christ came into the world and suffered and died on the cross for our sins. We broke His commandments; He paid the fine. Then He rose from the dead and defeated death, so that we could repent (turn from our sins and turn to God) and be saved.

Why not give your life to Christ now? The Bible tells us that God is not willing that any should perish, but that all should come to repentance. If you repent and put your faith in Jesus Christ as Lord and Savior, God will give you everlasting life.

If you are ready to turn from sin and put your faith in Jesus, pray something like this:

Dear Jesus, I am a sinner. I have broken your commandments. If I died as I am, I would be guilty and end up in hell. Your Word says if any one comes to you, you will not cast them aside. I ask you now, forgive me of all my sins. Be my Lord, and my Savior. I renounce all of my past. Fill me with your Holy Spirit. Show me your will for my life. In your precious name... Amen.

If you have prayed that prayer for the first time or if you are a backslider coming back to God, write me for a free book on how you can grow as a new Christian. When you write, be sure to include your prayer requests!! Write to:

Mike Smalley
Worldreach Ministries
P. O. Box 99
Rockwall, TX 75087
or e-mail us at revjms@hotmail.com

Visit our web site at www.world-reach.net

BIBLIOGRAPHY

Chapter 2

Leonard Ravenhill, *Why Revival Tarries* (Minneapolis, Bethany House Publishers, 1959).

Chapter 7

F. Nolan Ball, *God's Plan for Financing the Ministry* (Panama City, Florida, The Rock of Panama City, 1992).

Chapter 11

Ray Comfort, *The Evidence Bible* (Gainsville, Florida, Bridge Logos, 2001).

NOTES

NOTES

NOTES

NOTES

NOTES

NOTES

NOTES

NOTES

NOTES

NOTES

NOTES

NOTES

NOTES

ORDER FORM

QTY.	TITLE	PRICE	TOTAL
	Revival Fires Series (3 Tapes)	$15.00	
	Effective Evangelism 101 (a 6-tape soul-winning series)	20.00	
	How to Pray for an Evangelist	5.00	
	How to Live Life and Not Sin	5.00	
	A Fresh Visitation from Jesus	5.00	
	Knowing the Time	5.00	

Sub-Total _____

In U.S., add 10%. In Canada, add 20% to cost and 20% shipping _____

Enclosed is my seed faith gift for your ministry _____

Total Amount Enclosed

Sorry, no C.O.D.'s

Please charge my: ❑ VISA ❑ MasterCard ❑ Discover

☐☐☐☐☐☐☐☐☐☐☐☐☐☐☐☐ ☐☐-☐☐

Card Number   Expiration Date

Name: _____

Address: _____

City: _____ State: _____ Zip: _____

Daytime Phone: (____) _____

Signature: _____

To mail this form, or for a complete list of other books,
tapes and tracts by Mike Smalley, write to:

Worldreach Ministries
P. O. Box 99, Rockwall, TX 75087

or, visit us on the web at
www.world-reach.net